The PURPLE STORM

E.M.WILKIE

THE
PURPLE STORM

Aletheia Adventure Series Book 2

E M Wilkie

JOHN RITCHIE LTD
CHRISTIAN PUBLICATIONS

Copyright © 2014 by John Ritchie Ltd.
40 Beansburn, Kilmarnock, Scotland

www.ritchiechristianmedia.co.uk

ISBN-13: 978 1 909803 77 0

Written by E M Wilkie
Illustrated by E M Wilkie
www.aletheiabooks.co
Copyright © 2014

Cover illustration by Graeme Hewitson.
Interior illustrations are by E M Wilkie.

Unless otherwise indicated, Scripture quotations are taken from:
The Holy Bible, New King James Version®.
© 1982 by Thomas Nelson, Inc. Used by permission. All rights reserved.

To Zach,

This second adventure was written for your birthday, 2014,

with lots of love.

"God is our refuge..."

Psalm 46:1

PREFACE

This story is an attempt to help and encourage young readers to develop an understanding of the truth contained in the Word of God, the Bible. However, all characters, places, descriptions and incidents are entirely fictional and this adventure story is not intended to be a substitute for the teaching contained in the Bible, but rather an aid to understanding. The illustrations and allegories used in this story are not perfect; and therefore, whilst it is hoped that readers will benefit from the truth and lessons developed in this story, they must be urged to develop an understanding of Bible truth and doctrine from the Bible alone.

The author would like to acknowledge the invaluable help and advice of the following people:

M J Wilkie, R Hatt, A Henderson, and R Chesney.

Contents

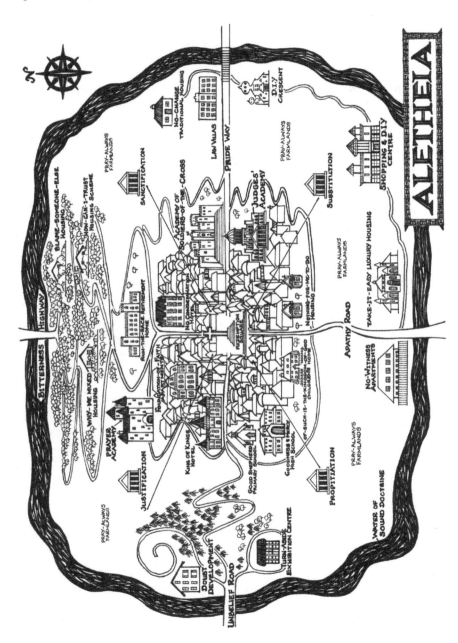

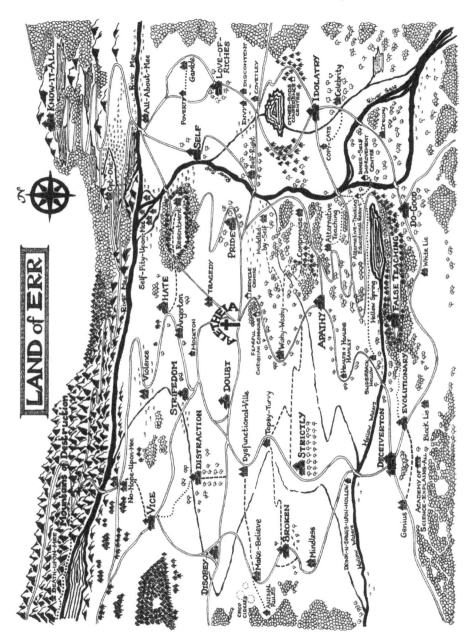

CHAPTER 1
AUTUMN WEEK

There was a touch of frost glistening in the shadows of Aletheia. Henrietta Wallop leaned over the balcony and peered down into the street far below. She could see the familiar sight of the Fruit-of-the-Spirit shops clustered at the edge of the narrow road. Already Mrs De Voté was opening her 'Faithful' shop, pausing to rub at an imaginary spot on the sparkling glass of the front window. This morning Mrs De Voté was wearing a bright red knitted scarf in addition to her tidy dress and apron.

You could almost tell the weather by what Mrs De Voté was wearing when she inspected her shop early in the morning. The cosy red scarf showed that summer was over and the chill of autumn had come.

From her vantage point, which was the top floor balcony of Foundation-of-

Faith Apartments, Henrietta could see south and east across the city of Aletheia. The city was perched at the top of a hill, and, all around the ancient buildings, the Pray-Always Farmlands spread out like a patchwork quilt. The trees were touched with the gold and orange hues of autumn. The land was harvested and bare. In the barns of the farm buildings dotted here and there were supplies stored for the winter ahead. The Pray-Always farmers would supply food to the city of Aletheia. It was important that the people had good things to eat, and only food grown on the Pray-Always Farmlands was watered with the Water of Sound Doctrine and safe for the people of Aletheia.

Beyond the farmlands, encircling the whole of Aletheia, was the Water of Sound Doctrine. The depth of the water had never been fathomed; the quality of the water had never been completely understood. But it was the only safe drinking water in the entire land of Err. If you didn't like the water you knew that the problem was inside of you and not in the wonderful, mysterious Water of Sound Doctrine.

It was very early in the morning when Henrietta was looking over the city of Aletheia, but she had a very good reason for being awake. Today marked the start of Autumn Week: a much anticipated treat when, instead of going to school, all the children in her class spent the entire week learning about one of the real-life jobs in Aletheia and doing important, interesting things instead of lessons. Henrietta could hardly understand why the whole city wasn't buzzing with excitement on this special morning but there was almost no traffic on the roads that she observed from the balcony. She could see the straight, steep road of Pride Way which was east, and down the gently sloping Apathy Road which led south. There were two other roads which ran in and out of the city of Aletheia: Unbelief Road to the west and Bitterness Highway to the north. Henrietta had never left the city by either of those difficult roads, but she had, once, walked down easy Apathy Road and out into the land of Err. That had been a few weeks ago, at the start of the summer. Henrietta and her twin brother, Hugo, and their youngest brother, Hezekiah, had set off on a trip with their friend Jack Merryweather, to rescue a boy called Timmy Trial[1]. The journey had turned into quite an adventure, and whilst Hugo and Henrietta had got into trouble over the trip, Henrietta still had a longing to go out into Err. They had learned about rescuing and helping people in Err on their previous trip; and Henrietta wanted to do more.

Hugo joined Henrietta on the balcony. He was in his pyjamas and rubbed his eyes sleepily.

"Just think," said Henrietta, "we might actually be going to the Academy *this very day*, learning all the secrets of real Rescuers!" Henrietta pointed to the turrets and towers of a massive, ancient fortress that the twins could see across the rooftops of the city of Aletheia. This was the Academy of Soldiers-of-the-Cross.

"We probably won't learn *all* of the secrets of the Rescuers, Henry," said Hugo. He was more realistic and cautious than his twin.

"We might actually get to go on a real rescue mission into Err!"

"I don't think so, Henry," said Hugo.

"But we just *might*," said Henrietta.

"Well, first we need to be chosen to do our Autumn Week at the Academy," Hugo reminded her.

"I should think they'll at least let us do that!" said Henrietta. "They know how badly we want to be real Rescuers!"

"Teachers are funny about these things sometimes," said Hugo wisely.

"Teachers are just funny full stop!" retorted Henrietta.

"But they're still the ones who decide things about us," said Hugo.

"If we *do* get to do our Autumn Week at the Academy of

Soldiers-of-the-Cross, what would be your most *favourite* thing to do?" asked Henrietta. "You know, if you could do absolutely anything a Rescuer could do?"

"Fly a Rescue Capsule," said Hugo. If there was one thing that Hugo longed to do it was to have even one short ride in the round, light aircraft that zipped across the sky, the aircraft that was known in Aletheia as a Rescue Capsule. This fascinating machine was used by the Rescuers of the Academy of Soldiers-of-the-Cross to go and help people in need.

Henrietta groaned. "I might have known you would want to do something with a Rescue Capsule," she said.

"Why did you ask then?"

"I suppose if we got to ride in a Capsule we could at least see interesting parts of Err from the sky," conceded Henrietta.

"Did you know that Capsules convert light into energy to fly?" said Hugo.

"Only because you've told me a million times before," said Henrietta.

"A million times!" exclaimed Hugo. "I probably only told you *once* if you're lucky!

"I wonder what happens if there's lightning and thunder," said

Henrietta. "Do you think the Rescue Capsule shoots straight into space and lands on another planet?"

"I hardly think so, Henrietta!" said Hugo in his best imitation of their teacher.

Henrietta giggled. Then, "They *will* let us go to the Academy for Autumn Week, won't they, Hugo?" she said seriously.

"I should think so," said Hugo. "And we've only got about… two hours before we find out for sure!"

Hugo and Henrietta Wallop had never gone to school as eagerly as they did the first morning of the all-important Autumn Week. They ate their breakfast, and, feeling very excited and important, they dressed in casual clothes and not in their usual school uniform. They set off for school earlier than they ever had before.

"I think I read that, in an emergency, Rescue Capsules *might* be able to use Water of Sound Doctrine as fuel," said Hugo, still thinking about his beloved Capsules as they walked down the narrow street from their home at Foundation-of-Faith Apartments.

"*Might* doesn't sound too reassuring," said Henrietta.

"It's something the Academy are researching," said Hugo.

"I should think *anything* would run on the Water of Sound Doctrine," said Henrietta. "They should just try it and see!"

"It's not as straightforward as that, Henry," said Hugo. "There are tests and experiments… Oh, good morning, Mr Forbear." Hugo broke off to greet a small, round, beaming man who was standing in the morning sunshine. Mr Forbear owned a store in the Fruit-of-the-Spirit shopping parade and he always stopped what he was doing to talk to anyone passing by. He smiled at the children.

"Well, well, you're two very early birds this morning!" he said.

"We've got Autumn Week this week," said Hugo.

"Yes, I know," said Mr Forbear. "I've got a student from your class coming to help me in my shop! I'm going to get lots of cleaning out and reorganising done this week!"

"Oh," said Henrietta. She looked at the small, cluttered 'Patience' shop. Mr Forbear had stuff absolutely everywhere but he never seemed to mind how long it took him to find something that a customer needed. He sold nails and screws, and hammers and tools, and all sorts of bits and pieces you might just need to repair your home. Sometimes it appeared that Mr Forbear was trying to find a tiny, individual, exactly-right-for-the-job nail in the corner of his crowded shop. And his customers just had to learn patience while they waited for him to find what they needed. "Do you know who is coming to help you in your shop this week, Mr Forbear?" asked Henrietta. She knew that the shopkeepers and other workers in Aletheia already knew the names of the schoolchildren who were assigned to them for Autumn Week.

"A girl called Hilda Hasty is coming to help me," said Mr Forbear.

"Oh!" said Henrietta, and then, "Ow!" as Hugo pinched her arm. "I wasn't going to say anything!" she exclaimed as they said goodbye to Mr Forbear and walked further down the narrow street. "But it must be some kind of joke putting the most impatient, moody girl in the whole school on work experience with Mr Forbear – who must be the most patient man in Aletheia!"

"I don't think Hilda's exactly the most impatient girl in the whole school," said Hugo who was not prone to exaggeration.

"But you know what I mean!" said Henrietta.

"Well, maybe that's *why* they've put Hilda to work in the

Patience shop," said Hugo.

"It still seems like a bad joke on Mr Forbear," said Henrietta. "He'll have a rotten week, poor man...!"

"Uh, hello, Mrs De Voté," said Hugo, interrupting his sister.

Mrs De Voté was stood outside of her Faithful shop, resting on a broom which she had evidently been using to sweep the pavement. "You're nice and early, dears," she said. She was a very old lady, but she still opened her shop every day, no matter the weather. Her shop opened before any other in Aletheia, and closed last of all. Henrietta had often seen a light in the window of the Faithful shop from the balcony of Foundation-of-Faith Apartments.

"Are you getting a student to help you this week, Mrs De Voté?" asked Henrietta.

"Oh no, dear," said the old lady. "I usually manage myself."

"Uh, yes," said Henrietta.

"And where are you spending your Autumn Week?"

"We don't know yet," said Hugo.

"But we're really hoping we're going to the Academy of Soldiers-of-the-Cross!" said Henrietta.

"That's always a popular choice," said Mrs De Voté. "But the front line can be a dangerous place for a Christian, and as many are needed faithfully behind the lines as at the front of them. Remember, rescuing begins at home."

"Well...yes..." said Hugo awkwardly.

"Uh...I hope you have a nice day," said Henrietta, and on they went, through the narrow, crooked streets of the old city, to Goodness and Mercy High School.

"What did Mrs De Voté mean about behind the lines and in front of them?" asked Henrietta.

"I think she means that stuff like prayer cover is important to support Rescuers who are going out to fight," said Hugo. "You know, people staying behind to pray and support the people doing the dangerous stuff."

"Like Mr Duffle praying when we went to rescue Timmy," said Henrietta. Mr Duffle was an exceedingly old man; but his prayers had proved more effective in the rescue of Timmy Trial[1] than any of the things the children had managed to do for Timmy.

"I feel kind-of bad about old ladies like Mrs De Voté who don't get any help during Autumn Week," said Henrietta with a sigh.

"Well, *you* can always help her to keep shop for a week," said Hugo.

"I don't see why it should be me!" said Henrietta. "Why do girls always have to do that sort of thing?"

"I didn't exactly say that it was only girls who did that sort of thing," said Hugo.

"Well," responded Henrietta, "you'd look very nice yourself in a neat apron, watering her plants, making cups of tea, and buttering scones, and..." She giggled as Hugo tried to trip her up. "On second thought, you don't make very good tea!" she said.

18 The Purple Storm

CHAPTER 2
JOSIE'S REQUEST

All of the children in Hugo and Henrietta's class at school had completed a form about where they would like to spend Autumn Week. There were plenty of interesting things they could do:

1. ***Judges' Academy****: learn about the laws of Aletheia and the land of Err, and how these are enforced;*

2. ***Keepers of the Water of Sound Doctrine****: learn how the Water of Sound Doctrine is protected and kept unpolluted, clean and balanced;*

3. ***Run-the-Race Retirement Complex****: learn about how to care for the elderly of Aletheia and about their special part in supporting the city;*

4. ***Pray-Always Farms****: help the farmers to sort through their crops and tend the animals of the Pray-Always farms;*

5. ***Prayer Academy****: visit the Academy and see the power of prayer at work;*

6. ***Aletheia Schools****: help the teachers at the Good Shepherd Primary School and the Goodness and Mercy High School;*

7. **Academy of Soldiers-of-the-Cross**: *visit the Academy and find out all about the work of the Rescuers of Aletheia;*

8. **City Contamination**: *see the City Contamination crews at work as they clear pollution and search for unclean invaders of the city of Aletheia;*

9. **Of-such-is-the-Kingdom-of-God Children's Home**: *help out at the children's home in Aletheia;*

10. **Aletheian Hotels**: *learn the secrets of serving people in one of the Aletheian Hotels;*

11. **Aletheian Shops**: *help in one of the city's shops and learn shop-keeping skills;*

12. **Roads and Transport:** *find out all about keeping the way to the cross clear for people who have come to worship and people who are seeking;*

13. **Redemption Square:** *work with the people who tend and guard the most important place in the city of Aletheia.*

There were more options too, but Hugo and Henrietta didn't need to look at all of the options for Autumn Week. They already knew what they wanted to do. They both ticked number 7 on the list in thick, dark pencil, so it couldn't possibly be mistaken for anything else. They didn't bother with second or third options as they were advised. They only wanted to work with the Rescuers of Aletheia at the mighty fortress of the Academy of Soldiers-of-the-Cross and they both spent considerable time writing convincing arguments in the 'Other Comments' box on the form.

The 'Other Comments' box on the Autumn Week Application Form was the subject of some discussion between the twins. The box was large and ominously empty and seemed to require a lot of well-chosen, persuasive words to ensure that their week at the Academy might actually become reality.

"I don't think we should write exactly the same, Henry," said Hugo.

"If we both write the same, then they'll have to send us both there, won't they?" said Henrietta.

"Or neither of us," said Hugo gloomily.

"Well, I don't think I want to go without you anyway," said Henrietta. "Would you want to go without me?"

Hugo's hesitation was not reassuring to Henrietta.

"I can't believe you would want to go without me…!" began Henrietta.

"That's not exactly what I said, Henry," said Hugo. "In fact, I didn't actually say anything at all!"

"But you wouldn't really want to go without me, Hugo, I mean really and truly, you would want me to *be there*…!"

"That's not exactly the point," said Hugo, deftly avoiding his sister's need for reassurance which did not fit well with his notion of a calm, detached Rescuer.

"Well, I think we should at least put similar things…"

In the end they compromised on the use of some words and phrases. Hugo absolutely refused to be part of Henrietta's more flowery, dramatic statements.

"Really, Henry, I don't think they'll believe that you would actually die of unhappiness if you didn't go to the Academy!" he remonstrated.

"They don't *know* that," said Henrietta darkly. "*I* don't even know that for sure!"

"Just put 'be upset' or something less…well, less unrealistic," suggested Hugo.

"You have to make them realise *how much* it means to you!" urged Henrietta.

"Rescuers don't exaggerate and go on about such things," said

Hugo with dignity, not at all sure about this. But he didn't think his eldest, much admired brother, Harold, would ever say such crazy things. And Harold was training to become a Rescuer at the Academy.

By the time they had completed the Other Comments box their statements were more-or-less in sync. After all, they both had the same good reasons for wanting to spend Autumn Week with the Rescuers. Apart from the excitement and adventure they craved, they sincerely wanted to help reach people with the good news about the Lord Jesus; they both truly wanted to be part of rescuing.

Despite being early at school the morning the Autumn Week placements were announced, Hugo and Henrietta weren't the first to arrive at their classroom. Most of their friends had already arrived. Even their cousin, Josie Faithful, was there, and Josie said she didn't like Autumn Week. But then she didn't really like anything about Aletheia these days.

Josie was a pretty girl with fly-away red hair. She looked a bit like her cousin, Henrietta, except that her hair was a more fiery shade than Henrietta's auburn. Josie had always lived in

Aletheia and knew that the Lord Jesus had died so that people could be saved[2]. Her parents and brothers were all Christians[3]. But Josie wasn't a Christian. She was certain there were other ways to be happier and better places to live than Aletheia. She had posters on her bedroom wall of movie stars and singers and other people who were famous in the land of Err. They looked beautiful and rich and perfectly happy. Josie wanted to meet them and find out how she could be like that. She wanted to explore the land of Err.

Henrietta and Josie were not only cousins, but they were friends. They had both been brought up in Aletheia, and learned all about the message of the Bible. Both Hugo and Henrietta had become Christians when they trusted in the Lord Jesus. The Lord Jesus had saved them from the punishment for all the wrong things they had done, things that the Bible calls sin[4]. Now Hugo and Henrietta were interested in learning about rescuing other people and helping them understand how the Lord Jesus could save them. But Josie wasn't interested in things like that, and whilst Henrietta and Josie were still friends, now they often argued and disagreed.

That morning, the all-important morning of Autumn Week, Josie looked miserable.

"Cheer up, Josie," said Henrietta as she took her usual seat beside her in the classroom. "You might surprise yourself by having a good Autumn Week!"

"It's not that," said Josie.

"What's up?" asked Henrietta. Josie didn't often confide in Henrietta anymore, but this morning was different: Josie looked a bit desperate, even scared.

"It's about what I wrote on the Autumn Week Application Form," said Josie.

"What option did you choose?" asked Henrietta. She knew Josie didn't want to spend Autumn Week in Aletheia; she wanted to go to Err instead.

"I didn't like any of the options on the form!" said Josie.

"Well, I think we all know that by now," said Henrietta, as usual quickly losing patience with her exasperating cousin. "You've gone on and on about that for weeks!"

"Shut up, Henry," said Josie. "Just because you're so happy to be in Aletheia and go to your precious Academy of Rescuers…!"

"Whatever," said Henrietta. "But what *did* you put on the application form that you're so worried about?"

"Not exactly worried…" said Josie, looking exactly that.

"Whatever," said Henrietta.

"Don't *keep* saying that!"

"Alright, alright," said Henrietta. She looked out of the classroom window across the Pray-Always Farmlands which were still frosty in shady places. The sun was creeping higher in the sky. The colours of the fields and the trees were bright and beautiful in the sunshine. She could see cows grazing the last of the grass before they were put away into the big barns for the winter. A small dog and a large man wandered happily along the path close to the school. Autumn Week was ahead of them. All was well in Aletheia. Henrietta couldn't imagine what it must feel like to be Josie where nothing was right about Aletheia. Josie couldn't see the sunshine and the beauty of an autumn day. Josie didn't even like Autumn Week!

"I didn't exactly choose one of the options on the application form," Josie whispered at last. She was fiddling with the corner of her desk, looking away from Henrietta, desperate and miserable.

"What *did* you write on the form then?" asked Henrietta. "It can't be that bad!"

"I wrote in the 'Other Comments' box that I wanted to do hair design in the town of Celebrity in Err," said Josie.

It took some effort not to laugh out loud. Josie was becoming established as the class rebel, but this was possibly the maddest thing she had ever done.

"Whiskers himself reads those forms!" said Henrietta, not particularly helpfully.

"Well, thanks for that," said Josie. "I already knew that, actually!"

"What on earth possessed you to…?"

"Does it really matter right now?" snapped Josie.

"No," conceded Henrietta. Josie had plenty of admiring friends who weren't Christians and probably they had encouraged her to write 'hair design in Celebrity' on her Autumn Week Application Form.

"What shall I do?" Josie whispered desperately.

"Do?" Henrietta echoed helplessly. But she was spared trying to think of an answer for Josie. For, at that very moment, the formidable person of 'Whiskers' himself entered the classroom.

Henrietta Wallop afterwards commented that it would have been worth paying a great deal of money to see Mr Philologus Mustardpot's face when he read Josie's request to be a hairdresser in the land of Err. Mr Mustardpot, secretly known as 'Whiskers' by the children, was in charge of education in Aletheia and Chief Headmaster of the schools there. He made sure that the schools in Aletheia only taught what the Bible said. Mr Mustardpot was big and tall, with alarming whiskers and a very loud voice. All of the children were in awe of Mr Mustardpot, and although Josie had told herself that it didn't matter what Whiskers thought about her Autumn Week Application Form, now that she was sitting under his all-seeing gaze she did not feel remotely brave about the matter.

Josie pretended she didn't care when, instead of being given her Autumn Week assignment with the other children, she was summoned into Mr Mustardpot's office to talk about her request. She followed the formidable figure of Whiskers from the classroom and none of Josie's friends, who had laughed at her application form and encouraged her to write 'hair design', dared to laugh now. You didn't do any of those things in the presence of Mr Philologus Mustardpot. Mr

Mustardpot and a white-faced Josie departed the classroom and, with avid attention, the children listened to the list of jobs they were allocated to that week.

"Dusty Addle, to the Academy of Soldiers-of-the-Cross," said the teacher, Mrs Steady, reading from her list.

Hugo glanced across the classroom at Henrietta. One of the four precious Autumn Week places at the Academy had already gone, and to Dusty Addle of all children!

Dusty Addle came from the town of Topsy-Turvy in the land of Err. Topsy-Turvy was a place where everything was upside down. The children were in charge of the adults; the houses had roofs in the ground and doors at the top; the trees and plants were all upside down and only dry, ugly roots showed above the ground; the sun shone at night, and the moon shone during the day; no one was very sure where the rain came from – it seemed to come up from the ground and all around, like a big, broken, sprinkler system. There were usually only sweets to eat because the children decided what shops could be in the town. And because the children were in charge, they beat up anyone who visited that they didn't want there. Topsy-Turvy was really a very disagreeable place to live.

Dusty's parents had decided they should send their children to the other schools in the land of Err. Things were such a mess in the town of Topsy-Turvy that Dusty's parents wanted to see if there was a better way of doing things. One of Dusty's brothers, Tumble, was sent to the Strictly Training Academy, where they had strict rules about everything that you did; another brother, Webb, was sent to the Academy of Science-Explains-All where they thought that science could explain everything without believing in God. And Dusty was sent to the Goodness and Mercy High School in the city of Aletheia, and lived very comfortably at the Of-such-is-the-Kingdom-of-God Children's Home. Dusty wasn't a Christian. He didn't know anything about the Bible before he went to school in Aletheia. Now that he lived in Aletheia he knew the Bible said the Lord Jesus was the only way of salvation[5]. But Dusty was pretty sure he could manage without believing what the Bible said. There were plenty of people in Err that seemed to be able to live in peace without the Bible. Of course, it was clear that Topsy-Turvy had messed up, but there were other towns where things might be alright.

"Henrietta Wallop, to the Academy of Soldiers-of-the-Cross," said Mrs Steady, continuing to read from her list.

"Hurrah!" cried Henrietta in excitement.

The children laughed and Hugo grinned across the classroom at his sister. He was pleased that she, at least, had made it to the Academy for Autumn Week.

"Hilda Hasty, to Mr Forbear, at the Patience shop in the Fruit-of-the-Spirit shopping parade," said Mrs Steady, ignoring the excitement the assignments were causing in the classroom.

Hilda seemed cautiously optimistic. "I really wanted to work in a bakery," she whispered to her friend. "What does Mr Forbear sell?"

Henrietta bit back a giggle. She was so ridiculously happy that she was going to the Academy of Soldiers-of-the-Cross for Autumn Week that anything and everything might have made her laugh. And the thought of grumpy Hilda Hasty grubbing around on the floor, trying to find tiny nails in the corner of Mr Forbear's shop, when all she wanted to do was eat cakes in a bakery, was really very funny.

"Hugo Wallop…"

Henrietta held her breath. Autumn Week would not be right without Hugo sharing it.

"…to the Academy of Soldiers-of-the-Cross," said Mrs Steady, and Henrietta slumped on her desk, too relieved to even express her excitement.

They were both going to the massive, mysterious stone fortress for Autumn Week. Nothing had ever been quite so perfect.

CHAPTER 3
DUSTY ADDLE

Hugo and Henrietta set off from Goodness and Mercy High School to walk to the Academy of Soldiers-of-the-Cross. The last frost of the morning had disappeared in the warm sunshine and already the sun was high in the sky. It seemed to them that too much of the morning had been wasted at school getting assigned their Autumn Week placements. All the twins wanted was to be at the Academy, learning the secrets of the Rescuers. Henrietta would have preferred to be alone with Hugo at the beginning of this perfect week, but Dusty Addle was with them too.

Dusty was tall for his age, with a good-natured face, and thick-rimmed glasses that gave him a clever, earnest appearance. He *was* actually clever but he always appeared to be muddled, as if all of his cleverness was tucked away somewhere behind his own funny ideas. Dusty had ideas about pretty much everything. He was certain he would find peace and happiness and riches in the land of Err. He didn't seem to understand what the Bible taught no matter how many times he was told.

"How come you're at school in Aletheia, Dusty?" asked Hugo as they walked along.

"Mr Mustardpot visited Topsy-Turvy and told everyone about Aletheia schools and education," said Dusty.

Hugo and Henrietta were only dimly aware of what Mr Mustardpot did when he was away from the school. It was surprising to learn that he went into Err to recruit children to come to school in Aletheia.

"They pelted him with mud," Dusty said matter-of-factly.

"Mr Mustardpot! What?! Who did?" exclaimed Henrietta.

"The children of Topsy-Turvy," said Dusty. "They pelted Mr Mustardpot with mud."

"Really?!" asked Hugo.

None of the children in Aletheia would ever have imagined anyone daring to throw mud at Mr Philologus Mustardpot.

"They always do stuff like that," said Dusty. "At least it wasn't stones this time."

"Why don't their parents stop them?" asked Henrietta.

"The children are in charge in Topsy-Turvy," said Dusty.

"Wow!" said Henrietta. She tried to imagine what that might be like. Good? Bad? Or just plain crazy...?

"Why are they in charge?" asked Hugo.

"Topsy-Turvy was supposed to be the perfect town," said Dusty.

"Because they put children in charge?" exclaimed Henrietta.

"Don't keep interrupting, Henry," said Hugo.

Dusty grinned good-naturedly. After living in Topsy-Turvy, nothing bothered Dusty. "I think the idea was that if you put children in charge, and gave them only nice things, and never taught them anything bad or wrong, then the children would be perfect and nice and the town would be perfect and nice too. Only it didn't work like that." That was a bit of an understatement. But after living in Aletheia for a while when he was at school, Dusty realised that the children here would have no idea how truly awful Topsy-Turvy had now become. It was really in a state of war. Gangs of children ruled the streets and picked on people they didn't like. People did not dare to go outside alone: they went out in groups for safety, because they were all afraid.

But Dusty clung on to the hope that somewhere else in Err there was a town that had got things just right. People were clever. Many people were good. Somewhere, someone must have found the answer to a good and peaceful life.

"But it wouldn't work putting children in charge!" said Henrietta. "The Bible tells us that!"

"Does it?" asked Dusty in surprise.

"The Bible says there's nothing good inside us," said Hugo. "That's why the town of Topsy-Turvy has gone so wrong, because everyone is wrong from the inside out[6]. That's why kids do wrong without anyone teaching them to!"

"Do you really think that's why?" asked Dusty. "I think that people have all sorts of good bits inside them that just need to be found."

"Did your parents send you to Aletheia so that you could learn how to become a Christian?" asked Hugo.

Dusty shrugged. "I don't know," he said. "I think they just want to know if there's a better way of doing things. Better than Topsy-Turvy, that is."

"Well, of course there is," said Henrietta. "That's why Aletheia is the best place in the whole of Err, because it's the place that teaches the Truth of the Bible! So it *is* the right way of doing things."

"Perhaps there is more than one truth," said Dusty peaceably. Dusty's ideas didn't always make sense but he was very nice about them.

"That's rotten bananas," said Henrietta. "Then the truth wouldn't be truth at all! It would only be an idea, or a suggestion or something!"

"Well, perhaps there are lots of ways to be happy," said Dusty. "You know, different ways for different people. Perhaps it's inside us all along and we just have to learn what suits us best. I don't think people are really all bad."

Henrietta rolled her eyes. It didn't make any sense to her that Dusty couldn't see what the Bible said was the Truth. If there was any other way to be right, would the Lord Jesus have needed to die on the cross? There was no other way to be right before God; the Lord Jesus was the only way![5] It seemed odd to be going on Autumn Week to learn about the Rescuers with Dusty – when Dusty needed rescuing himself! What was it that Mrs De Voté had said? "*Rescuing begins at home.*" Was it possible their work at the Academy that week would involve rescuing Dusty?

The three children reached the Academy of Soldiers-of-the-Cross. The massive stone walls and towers and turrets rose high above them. A flag showing a white cross fluttered from the central tower.

Somehow the Academy looked different today. Hugo and Henrietta had seen the fortress plenty of times before, and they had even been inside it once or twice. But today everything seemed more important. Slowly they all began to walk up the wide steps to the huge open entrance.

"I wonder if we'll have our own office this week," said Henrietta in a suitably hushed, awed tone.

"I shouldn't think so, Henry," said Hugo.

Rescuers in uniform walked confidently up and down the steps, starting the business of the day. Some of them looked fierce and battle-scarred; all of them seemed big and important. Dusty looked amazed at the fortress and the men and women who had business there.

"Awesome!" he said.

Henrietta clutched Hugo's arm in excitement and then quickly let go when she remembered they were there on 'official' business and ought to know what they were doing.

They entered the Academy through the massive open doorway. Before them was the gigantic entrance hall with impressive suits of armour lining the stone walls. The quick footsteps of busy Rescuers echoed around, clattering purposefully on the shiny marble floor. There were corridors and rooms in every direction. The vaulted ceiling seemed to rise to the sky. There were small glass panes in the high roof through which the autumn sun shone brightly, casting the shadow of a cross on the marble floor. Everyone but them seemed to know in which direction they were to go and exactly what they ought to be doing.

"Awesome!" said Dusty again.

Feeling excited and important the three children stepped past the large screens which stood inside the Academy, close to the entrance. The screens were shiny metal and glass; everyone who entered the Academy had to pass them and no one paid them any attention at all.

But then something happened.

The silent, slowly flashing 'Contamination Detector' sign on the screens changed. The green smiley face transformed suddenly to a red scowl and the most terrific noise screeched out around them. Loud, jarring buzzing shattered the morning calm.

'*Contamination Alert!*' '*Contamination Alert!*' flashed on and off the screens in big red writing that Hugo was certain everyone in Aletheia could see.

And from all around, Rescuers descended on them.

CHAPTER 4
CONTAMINATION!

Hugo thought the awful *Contamination Alert* alarm would never stop. Actually it was quickly hushed by a grey-haired man who wore a shirt with a missing button and had a half-eaten bacon roll in one hand. He didn't look as if he was capable of dealing with any contamination, whether real or imagined. But the several Rescuers who appeared when the alarm sounded melted away at his presence and left the three children with the grey-haired man. The man ushered them to a small door by the entrance which said 'Security'.

"It's Autumn Week, isn't it?" the man said cheerfully. He put his half-eaten bacon roll on his small desk and smiled at the children.

"Yes, sir," said Hugo, mortified that their grand entrance into the Academy of Soldiers-of-the-Cross had been interrupted by that awful alarm.

"The school usually lets me know who's coming," said the man. "Then I can stop the alarm, you see? Well, never mind. We'll get you sorted in a jiffy!"

"Why did the alarm go off like that?" asked Dusty.

"It goes off if it detects contamination," said the man.

"But we're not contaminated," said Henrietta. "Ow!" she glared at Hugo. "What did you do that for?"

Hugo was making all sorts of signs which were intended to hush his sister. He had been reading about the Academy of Soldiers-of-the-Cross and he knew about the Contamination Detector at the entrance. Hugo could guess why the alarm had sounded. The alarm sounded when someone posed a potential threat to the important work of the Academy. For example, when someone carried some sort of contamination into the fortress with them. The contamination might be one of the creatures of Err. People could be shadowed by a Snare, or be carrying a tiny Meddler in their clothing or hair, or be trailing a Stumble from their foot, or have the cloud of a Sloth about them, and other things besides. If people didn't want to believe in the Truth of the Bible, well then, they would attract other things into their lives instead.

Thankfully the security man appeared calm and unconcerned. He picked up a book-shaped object – which looked like a Bible – from an overflowing shelf. Most of his small office was overflowing but it was also cheerful and not at all alarming for a security office. The room was a round shape, the walls were stone, and there was a lovely little fire crackling in a stone fireplace.

"It's my first fire of the year," said the man as he moved the book slowly up and down and around Hugo. "I'm usually lighting my fire about the time of Autumn Week. They say it's going to be a hard winter ahead!"

"Is it?" asked Henrietta with interest. "I hope that means we get snow for Christmas!"

"You wouldn't like the snow in Topsy-Turvy," commented Dusty. He watched the man move the book slowly around Henrietta too. It seemed that the book was checking the children for the contamination that the big screens had detected. Dusty wasn't looking forward to his turn. He had a horrible feeling that he had somehow carried contamination into this marvellous Academy. The book-shaped thing didn't seem at all concerned at either Hugo or Henrietta, so the problem must be *him!*

"You should ask the folks in the Control Room about the weather forecast," said the man.

"I've read about the Control Room!" said Hugo.

"He's read *all* about the Academy," said Henrietta. "Hundreds of books!"

"Not hundreds, Henry," said Hugo.

"Quite right, son," said the man. "You'll make a grand Rescuer if you go into the thing thoroughly!"

Henrietta was trying to see the interesting screens behind the man's desk. On one screen there appeared to be a very complex layout of the entire fortress with a multitude of different coloured dots moving about. She was just about to ask what it all meant when there was a distinct buzz. It happened when the security man passed the book around Dusty. The man quickly scribbled something on the pad of paper on his desk.

"I'm afraid I didn't wash much this morning," said Dusty looking embarrassed. "I sort of ran out of time."

"I don't think it's to do with washing," said Henrietta, but she sounded slightly doubtful as she said it and quickly stepped out of reach of Hugo who was trying to send her another silent message and seemed to be on the verge of pinching her again.

"Don't you worry about not washing, son," the man said kindly.

"I didn't wash much this morning either," said Hugo.

"Yeugh! Hugo! That's disgusting!" exclaimed Henrietta.

"Girls need to wash more than boys, don't they, Dusty?" said Hugo.

"What's wrong with me and not the others?" asked Dusty. "Why am I contaminated?"

"There's nothing wrong with you that the Lord Jesus can't wash away and put right if you'll trust in Him,[7]" said the man. "The other two have been cleansed by the Lord Jesus, that's why they're not contaminated, you see?"

"Oh," said Dusty.

"Here at the Academy we don't concentrate on what's contaminating a person," said the man, "we like to focus on the answer to all of our problems. And that's the Lord Jesus. He did not come into the world to condemn the world and point out all the problems, but He came so that the world through Him could be saved[8]."

A discreet knock sounded on the door and Hugo and Henrietta's eldest brother, Harold Wallop, poked his head around the door. Harold Wallop was training to be a Rescuer at the Academy of Soldiers-of-the-Cross. The twins were very proud of Harold, although they had mixed feelings about the prospect of having his eyes on them during Autumn Week. Harold knew them too well and he might not feel inclined to trust them with responsibilities that the twins felt more than able to bear. But right now they were very pleased to see him, and looking so smart in his uniform too.

"I wondered where you'd got to!" said Harold. He grinned at the twins and Dusty. "Are they all set to go, Jeff?" he asked the man.

"All set!" replied Jeff.

"It was me, I set the alarm off," said Dusty, still a bit embarrassed at the alarm, and extra embarrassed at having admitted in front of Henrietta that he hadn't washed much that morning. All the boys at school thought that Henrietta Wallop was pretty cool, and Dusty was no exception. He was very grateful to Hugo for trying to make him feel better about it all and saying that he didn't wash much either.

"Don't worry about setting the alarm off, Dusty," said Harold. "It's really the school's fault for not having warned us. The Academy is usually ready for visitors."

"Just what I said," said Jeff.

"Are you looking after us this week, Harold?" asked Henrietta.

"Me, and Bourne too," said Harold. He tweaked Henrietta's

hair. He was well aware of the twins' mixed feelings about his supervision that week, but the added presence of Bourne Faithful was likely to soften the blow.

Bourne Faithful was a cousin of Hugo and Henrietta, and Josie's oldest brother. He was already a *Lieutenant* at the Academy. Most of the children in Aletheia knew how great Bourne was. He had a rugged, fierce appearance and an interesting scar across his cheek. The children liked to imagine that Bourne had come by this heroic-looking mark in a fight with a fierce and deadly foe. But Bourne never talked about his scar and his silence on the matter only made it an object of even more wonder.

Henrietta was mostly pleased that her brother and cousin were responsible for them that week. There had been the faint hope that someone completely unknown might be assigned to show them around and explain things. Someone, if there was anybody left, who had not heard about their ill-fated adventure in the land of Err[1] and that might just trust them to take another trip there. But, on the whole, her oldest brother and much admired cousin were a pretty good deal.

Harold led them from the cosy security office into the marble hallway. Jeff followed them and saluted them goodbye with his half-eaten bacon roll. "I recommend the bacon rolls from the Refreshment Hall!" he called after them.

The children followed Harold past the suits of armour and across a big shiny plaque in the middle of the floor. The plaque said, 'Peace I leave with you'.[9] It was part of a verse from the Bible.

"That's an odd thing to put in a fortress of soldiers," remarked Dusty. "I thought soldiers went to war!"

"We are engaged in warfare, but only to proclaim the peace that is available to those who place their faith in the Lord Jesus,[10]" said Harold. "It is only in finding peace with God that people can have any real peace in their lives."

Dusty thought about his own search for peace and happiness for himself and his family. There certainly wasn't peace in Topsy-Turvy, where they had tried to make a perfect town by assuming there was good in everyone. He thought it might be found in another town in Err, perhaps through riches, or by doing good, or by some other means. But was it possible that real peace was only found in God, through this thing called *faith* in His Son the Lord Jesus?

"What exactly is faith?" asked Dusty.

"Faith[11] simply means trusting in someone or something. True faith is only in God[12] and in the Word of God, which is the Bible. Faith is believing that what God says is true even if you can't see it or prove it."

"I suppose people trust in all kinds of things apart from God," said Dusty.

"Yes," agreed Harold. "They certainly do. But we ought only to have faith in God because He is the only One who has proved He can be absolutely trusted[13]. Faith in anything or anyone else is without substance and will end in disappointment and disaster."

"Oh," said Dusty. He looked puzzled at Harold's answer but just then Harold stopped at a door which was signed 'Relaxation Room'.

"We don't need to relax!" exclaimed Hugo, anxious to get on with the job of being a Rescuer.

"We're not stopping here for long," said Harold. "We're just meeting up with...uh, the other member of Autumn Week from your class."

"No one else was chosen to spend Autumn Week with the Rescuers," said Henrietta. "I think there must have been some mistake."

"No mistake," said Harold.

"Who is it?" asked Henrietta. "Who else is joining us for Autumn Week?"

"Remember, Henry, this week is about learning to rescue those in need," said Harold. "Try to remember that when dealing with…"

"Who? Why are you telling *me*?" asked Henrietta.

Harold opened the door to the Relaxation Room. Sitting on a couch, looking comfortable and reading a novel, was Josie Faithful.

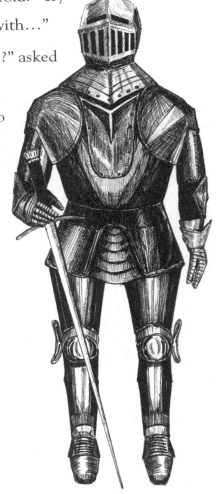

CHAPTER 5
THE STAIR-GOBBLER

Henrietta tried hard to remember what Harold had said to her about Josie being someone who needed to be rescued. It helped her to bite her tongue when they greeted Josie and recovered from the surprise that she was also spending Autumn Week at the Academy of Soldiers-of-the-Cross. Henrietta hoped that Josie wouldn't ruin the week for them all.

"Mr Mustardpot brought me here himself," explained Josie. "I arrived before any of you!"

"What did Whiskers say about your application for doing Autumn Week in Err?" asked Henrietta.

"That's private," said Josie.

"I don't know why you would want to spend Autumn Week in Err when you could be in this fortress," Dusty surprised them by saying. "It's pretty awesome here!"

"It's alright," said Josie graciously.

Henrietta concentrated on the interesting things in the room and tried not to snap at Josie. But if rescuing was about dealing with people who were as exasperating as Josie, and not so much about big, grand, exciting adventures, then clearly she had a lot more to learn about it.

"We might even get to go into Err," Josie was saying. "Bourne said so when I asked him."

"Really?" said Hugo. "We might truly get to go into Err on a mission or something?"

Henrietta looked across the room to where her cousin, Bourne, and her brother, Harold, were carrying on a quiet conversation about something which did not concern the children. Probably Bourne had talked about visiting Err to keep Josie quiet.

"We might as well take them with us to the Control Room," Bourne was saying. "We'll have to check the Storm Tracker to know for sure."

"A purple storm!" murmured Harold. "Are you sure Satchel Standfirm said a *purple* storm?"

"It was hard to hear through the crackling and interference," said Bourne. "I think Meddlers have been interfering with their Mission Link again. But we should get a further update in the next hour or so…"

"What's a purple storm?" Josie asked suddenly. She had been

forgotten in a conversation between Hugo and Dusty about Rescue Capsules and had tuned into her brother's conversation with her cousin Harold.

"A purple storm is a big storm," Bourne said briefly. "It's very unusual, but since we're going to show you the Central Control Room anyway, we'll check up on it and show you how our tracker systems work."

Hugo was out of his chair like a rocket.

"Awesome!" said Dusty.

Henrietta dashed to the door.

Josie put away her novel and slowly followed them.

The four children followed Bourne and Harold along winding corridors to the very heart of the massive fortress. Before them was the biggest, widest, highest winding staircase they could ever imagine. It seemed to go down, round and round and round and round, into the heart of the earth and darkness beneath them. And it rose into the very highest tower of the huge Academy, circling round and round, again and again, until it became quite small above them. Close to the inside rail of the staircase, almost invisible unless you knew where to look, were two tracks of parallel rails. Signs at frequent intervals on the staircase said "Keep clear of the rails."

"Awesome!" gasped Dusty. "Does it go down into the dungeons?"

Hugo and Henrietta exchanged glances. It was rumoured, amongst the children of Aletheia, that there were, indeed, dungeons at the Academy, and that prisoners were kept there. Hugo and Henrietta had never been able to discover the truth of the matter. Even Hugo's book about the Academy said nothing about dungeons or prisons. Harold only laughed at them when they had questioned him about the matter.

"That old story!" he said. "I heard that rumour when I was about your age too!"

"But he didn't actually deny it," Henrietta said to Hugo when they later discussed Harold's response. "He *didn't* say there *wasn't* a prison, or a dungeon, or both."

"I don't think it's likely, Henry," said Hugo.

But neither of the twins was convinced of the truth of the matter and the intriguing question remained. Hugo was glad that Dusty had asked the question. He wanted to know, but he didn't want Bourne or Harold to think he was stupid to be talking about the unknown dungeons.

"Dungeons?" said Bourne, considering Dusty's question with a twinkle in his eye. "I don't know about dungeons exactly, I've never seen all of the underground part of the Academy myself, so I guess I couldn't exactly say what's lurking there! But beneath the fortress are our emergency supplies and accommodation, in the case of all-out war."

All-out war had quite a thrilling sound to it.

"War?" echoed Josie. "Why would there be war?"

"We're already at war," said Harold. "There has been war in the world since the first man sinned."

"You mean Adam?" asked Dusty.

"Yes, I mean Adam,[14]" said Harold.

Dusty didn't say anything to that. Hugo and Henrietta knew that Dusty didn't believe in the Bible, but he didn't argue with Harold.

"But most of the towns in Err don't care about Aletheia," said Josie. "I mean, they're not interested in war at all, they all want peace!"

"Oh, well done, Josie," said Henrietta sarcastically. "Only you could tell real Rescuers about a place you've never even been to!"

"Shut up, Henry," said Josie.

Henrietta caught Harold's glance and tried to bite her tongue again.

"Topsy-Turvy is just like a war-zone!" said Dusty.

Josie usually liked Dusty's strange ideas about finding peace and happiness and riches somewhere in Err. She was as surprised as anyone when he agreed with Harold about war in Err.

"I mean," continued Dusty, "Topsy-Turvy somehow got things wrong about how to live and be happy and stuff, but there might be other places in Err that have got it right."

"I wouldn't be so sure about that," said Harold.

And then an awestruck silence suddenly descended amongst them.

Flying with great speed towards them was an incredible contraption. Round and round the bends at breathtaking speed it flew, barely seeming to touch the rails that it clutched with smooth runners.

"Awesome!" said Dusty. "Absolutely awesome!"

The other three were no less astonished than he. Even Hugo and Henrietta had never heard of the Stair-Gobbler of the Academy. Hugo wondered how many of the wonders of the mysterious fortress his textbook had left out.

"Good, isn't it?" said Harold.

"Wow," murmured Hugo.

"Good doesn't begin to describe it!" said Dusty. "Absolutely..."

"Awesome!" concluded Josie; even she cheered up at the sight of the Stair-Gobbler

"Climb aboard!" said Bourne. "Are you ready for the ride of your lives?"

If Hugo never got to ride in a Rescue Capsule during Autumn Week at the Academy, he thought he would be truly content just riding the Stair-Gobbler.

The long, rounded capsule stopped by the children and their two Rescuer guides. Silently the see-through cover opened. There were two seats in each row. The rows faced up the way if you were going up, and down the way if you were going down.

"You must put your seatbelts on," warned Bourne.

Bourne and Harold sat at the front, where there were surprisingly few controls. Hugo and Henrietta sat behind them; and Josie and Dusty at the back. They were all sitting on a very steep slope, looking up the endless winding staircase that rose above them.

"Awesome!" said Dusty, as the see-through roof silently closed over them. "Put your belt on, Josie!"

"I really don't see…" but whatever Josie was about to say was lost in her shriek of alarm. Bourne had pulled the lever around in a neat circle until their destination read, 'Central Control Room', and then pressed the big, shiny, green 'Go' button.

The Stair-Gobbler shot upwards at top speed, flinging them back in their seats, circling round and round the spiral staircase until they didn't know whether they were going right or left, this way or that, up or down, or whether they were even the right way up or on their heads. Josie continued to shriek loudly, Dusty kept saying "Awesome!" and Henrietta clutched Hugo's hand in sheer joy. Hugo sat silently, trying to take in the wonder of it all, trying to guess how many levels they had passed, and how close they were to the impossibly high ceiling. But he could only dimly imagine how high the tower with the spiral staircase rose, and how fast they were ascending the stairs. The Stair-Gobbler – or simply 'The Gobbler' as it was known by the Rescuers – was well named. It seemed to gobble up the stairs before them – so fast that they were gone before you'd seen the next one coming. It hardly seemed to connect to the rails; it simply flew.

All at once they stopped. They hurtled forward in their seats and Harold and Bourne leapt from the Gobbler as if they had barely felt the furious, stomach-churning ride. Hugo tried to leap out too, but his legs felt wobbly and he clutched hold of the handrail of the small landing place for a moment. Then he tried to look as unconcerned as his brother and his cousin. Josie was clutching her sides and looking wide-eyed and extremely pale. She looked as if she was just about to be sick and Bourne pointed to the 'Sick Here Please' bucket that stood close by.

"That's disgusting!" murmured Josie faintly. Somehow she managed to keep from being sick and placed her hand firmly over her mouth.

"It can actually be quite useful," said Bourne. "The Academy recycles all the sick at the Vomitorium."

"That's totally gross!" exclaimed Josie. "It should be illegal!"

Bourne chuckled. Hugo wondered if Bourne was teasing or if it could possibly be true. Everything about this Academy was so much more incredible than he had ever imagined; suddenly nothing seemed impossible. For a moment Hugo imagined the produce of the Vomitorium – if there really was such a thing –

being fed to the prisoners in the dungeons. But that didn't seem likely. The Academy was about rescuing and restoring people. What mysterious use could *sick* have...?

Dusty didn't seem at all put out at the suggestion of the Vomitorium. He was still saying "Awesome," and seemed largely unaffected by the motion of the Gobbler. Henrietta clutched Harold's arm in gratitude for such a wonderful ride. For a moment she forgot he was an important Rescuer and that they were on 'official' business in the Academy; for a moment he was merely her big brother and he had just shared the wildest ride of her life.

"Alright, Henry?" said Harold, with a grin.

"Alright!" she said enthusiastically. "Can we go right down in it next time too? Right down to the dungeons?"

Harold laughed.

"Ready, kids?" said Bourne. He watched as all four of them found their land legs and began to look around with interest.

Ahead of them was a massive, shiny metal door. From behind the door they could hear clicking and clacking and bubbling and popping and gurgling and murmuring and all sorts of other intriguing noises besides. The big silver letters on the door read, 'Central Control Room'. Underneath was a sign that said, 'Authorised Personnel Only.'

Feeling very important, the four children followed the Rescuers to the door.

CHAPTER 6
THE CENTRAL CONTROL ROOM

The important-looking Central Control Room door opened silently as the children approached. Immediately inside the door there was a circular balcony running around an enormous round chamber. That was all they observed to start with, but when the children walked to the balcony rail they could see exactly where the incredible sounds were coming from.

It was a fantastic scene. Below them was the most extraordinary variety of machines and instruments. They flashed and spun, went up and down, in and out, round and round, this way and that; they puffed coloured smoke, showed bright, multi-coloured lights, flung pieces of paper into stacked trays, and one even seemed to be snowing. Around the machines were people in bright coloured or patterned garments, like long coats. Each machine seemed to attract staff in different types of coats. They were reading dials, adjusting knobs, writing down numbers, and studying maps and diagrams. There were people in red coats, blue coats, green coats, yellow coats, orange coats, even in raincoats. Covering half of the massive circular wall of the lower chamber was a huge screen. It showed the entire land of Err in incredible detail. They could see dots for houses, and small leaves for trees; there were clouds, and rain, and in the far north, above the Mountains of Destruction, they could see snow falling. This screen was the central Mission Detector. It was connected to all of the individual Mission Detectors which Rescuers used to help them with their missions in Err. There were small dots with labels on the massive map. These were individual Rescuers going about their work across the land, telling the people of Err the good news about the Lord Jesus who could save them. The Central Control Room could see exactly where they all were at any time.

The four children stood in silence, trying to take it all in. Even Josie had nothing to say; she still looked pale from their wild ride on the Gobbler.

"I read about the Central Control Room in the 'History of the Rescuers' book I borrowed," said Hugo. "But there weren't any pictures and I never imagined anything like this!"

"It's quite something, isn't it?" agreed Harold.

"Awesome!" said Dusty.

"We're standing on the Observer Deck," said Bourne. "This

is where Rescuers come when they want some information, for example if they're preparing for a mission."

"They would never believe this in Topsy-Turvy," murmured Dusty. "All the machines in Topsy-Turvy are broken."

Hugo was looking at the flat, oblong screen attached to the railing, close to where they stood. There were similar screens at intervals all the way around the balcony.

"You just write your request on the communication screen, and then press 'send'," said Harold.

"Then it goes shooting down the tube," added Bourne.

They all peered over the edge to see clear, round tubes coming out of the screen and disappearing into the room below.

"And it goes to whichever machine, or machines, has the answer. And then you wait a short while and the answer comes back."

"Awesome!" said Dusty.

"Can we try it?" asked Henrietta.

"Ask about Celebrity!" said Josie. "Ask what the weather is or something like that!"

"What's happening in Topsy-Turvy?" asked Dusty.

"Ask something quite specific," suggested Harold. "If you ask a general question you'll only get a general answer."

Henrietta wrote, "What is the weather like in Topsy-Turvy?" on the screen with her finger.

"Now watch the folk in the green coats," said Harold. "They are the team that manage the Weather Guide machine over there."

They all looked at the team of people clustered around the Weather Guide. It was a strange contraption. It had shiny metal curves and supports sticking up in the air; in the middle of them was a big round, glass ball. A man in a green coat pulled a piece of paper from the tube next to the machine and read it.

"That's your request, Henry," said Bourne.

"Wow!" said Henrietta. "Look at them, Hugo! He's probably putting my request through those buttons below the big ball..."

"I can see it, Henry," said Hugo.

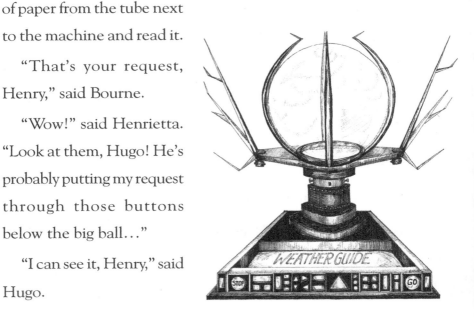

"We can all see it!" said Josie. She had at last regained some colour following the ride on the Gobbler. "I want to go next!" she said.

"Wait," said Harold. "Watch the Weather Guide."

As they watched there was a strange *whoosh* and water began flying in all directions inside the big, round, Weather Guide ball.

"Usually it's quite clear what the weather is," said Bourne. "But in Topsy-Turvy..."

"It looks weird," said Josie.

"That's how it rains in Topsy-Turvy," said Dusty.

"Spraying all around like that?" exclaimed Henrietta.

"You get wet everywhere," said Dusty.

"Umbrellas are no use in Topsy-Turvy!" said Harold.

"What's an umbrella?" asked Dusty.

"Can we ask something about a nice town now?" said Josie. "A town like Celebrity?"

"Wait," said Harold. "The results are coming back to us now."

Sure enough, the screen on the balcony by which they stood suddenly flashed to life. Across it the message said 'It's wet in Topsy-Turvy! Rain will continue to fall, rise, and spray from multiple directions for the next couple of days. There is little chance you will remain dry if on an outdoor mission; waterproof gear is advisable. Check with the Research and Development of Outdoor Equipment Department for any update on the specialist Topsy-Turvy Weather Gear they are developing. It may be available for your mission.'

"Boring," said Josie, despite the fact that Dusty was most interested in the development of 'Weather Gear' for Topsy-Turvy.

"What's that machine, over there?" asked Hugo. He pointed at a massive, complex device with countless tiny pipes going everywhere and a big central dial which had a bright orange splash across it.

"That's the Prayer Power Monitor," said Bourne. "That's a very important contraption!"

"You mean that thing records people praying to God?" asked Dusty.

"Prayer is our most valuable source of power," said Bourne. "We rely on God to work when we pray to Him."

"Why is it showing orange just now?" asked Henrietta.

"That coloured dial shows how much overall prayer power we have," said Harold. "Orange is 'Adequate' prayer. Really we want it to be on the dark green – which is enough prayer for a revival where many people get saved! But lots of Christians find it hard to spend time in prayer."

"You'd think they would pray if they believed in God enough," observed Dusty.

"Yes," agreed Bourne, "you would think that, wouldn't you?"

Josie had enough of waiting for her turn to send a request. She leaned forward and wrote, 'How is Melody from Celebrity?' She quickly pressed 'send' in case Harold or Bourne thought of stopping her. Melody was a very famous movie star who lived in Celebrity. Josie thought that Melody was beautiful and rich and must be the happiest person alive. Melody seemed to have everything anyone could possibly want to be very happy. She watched intrigued as several machines and bright coated teams received her message. The people in the coloured coats seemed perplexed by the request and looked up towards the balcony. Then they got to work on their various machines.

Bourne read his sister Josie's request. He didn't say anything. He just pointed at the various machines and explained what was happening.

"The Law Breaker is checking Melody's record," he said. "I

expect they'll find she's broken most of the Ten Commandments and plenty of other Aletheian laws besides."

Josie's mouth fell open but Bourne continued before she could protest.

"The Aletheia Alert equipment is at work detecting the danger level Melody poses to the city of Aletheia…"

"Danger level from Melody!" spluttered Josie. "She's never even been to Aletheia! And I don't suppose she ever will!"

"She is influencing people here nonetheless," said Bourne, "and I'm afraid you are one of them."

"One of my brothers fancies Melody," said Dusty rather unhelpfully.

"The Revealer Device is checking to see if any new invention, trend or evil we're not yet aware of is connected to Melody," Bourne continued.

"Evil!" exclaimed Josie.

"The Rascal Register is seeing how many of the creatures of Err are detected close to her and her home in Celebrity…"

"But that isn't what I meant at all!" said Josie. "I don't want to know those sorts of things about Melody!"

"But this is the truth," Bourne said soberly. "What we find out from this Control Room is the real truth about a person and what they are on the inside. It's not about what a person pretends to be to everyone else, or what they look like from the outside."

"Awesome!" said Dusty.

"I wish you would stop saying that!" snapped Josie. She was red faced and angry. "Tell them to stop searching!" she said. "I don't want to know anymore of those sorts of things!"

But neither Harold nor Bourne needed to tell the bright coated teams of people to stop searching for information about Melody the movie star. For suddenly a device they had not previously noticed came to life in the most extraordinary way. One moment the Storm Tracker was producing small amounts of vaguely coloured, pretty smoke clouds in the tall Storm Indicator Glass, and the next it had turned the most astonishing bright purple and sounded the most terrifying alarm. "*Alert! Alert! Alert!...*" came the screechy voice of the contraption.

From all around the room people descended on the Storm Tracker while other people began to frantically operate their machines.

The children put their hands over their ears, trying to shut out the frightening, wretched cry of '*Alert! Alert!*'

Harold Wallop and Bourne Faithful were pale with anxiety.

"Captain Steadfast is on duty," Bourne murmured to Harold. "He'll be on his way."

"Satchel Standfirm was right!" Harold exclaimed to Bourne. "It's a purple storm!"

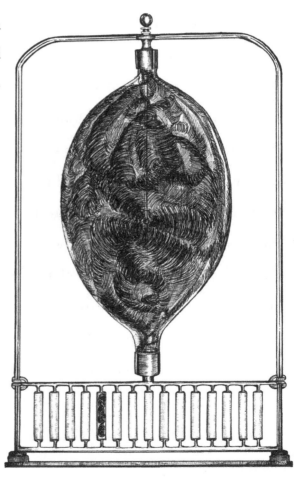

CHAPTER 7

MR STANDFIRM

The awful screech of '*Alert! Alert!*' continued to echo around the vast chamber and up to the balcony on which the children stood.

"I think we've had enough alarms for one day!" said Henrietta with her hands clapped tightly over her ears. How many other screeching, piercing alarms did the Academy hold?

Senior Rescuers with many gold stripes on their uniforms began to arrive on the balcony. For a moment the children were forgotten. A tall man strolled in and made his way to where Bourne and Harold stood. Hugo and Henrietta knew he was Captain Ready Steadfast, who was the Deputy Chief of all the Rescuers in the land of Err. Captain Steadfast was the most senior Rescuer on duty for emergencies and he immediately took charge.

"Can you quieten the 'Alert' alarm, Brian?" Captain Steadfast was speaking into a curious little tube that he had detached from the communication screen on the balcony. The children had not noticed it before, but it was clear that all the people who were hurrying between the machines in the room below could hear Captain Steadfast clearly.

The man called Brian appeared to be in charge of all the people who managed the big machines. He was a small, round man with large glasses and a big, bald head. He was the only person wearing a white coat, but, more remarkably, he was also wearing a homemade, bright orange, knitted cardigan over the top of his long coat. The cardigan had very large, orange buttons, and a startling array of colour around the edge, as if 'Mrs Brian' had run out of wool and added all the odd bits from her knitting bag in order to finish the cardigan.

Brian gave quick instructions – accompanied by a lot of gestures and hand waving – to the team of people in matching raincoats who were seeking to quieten the Storm Tracker. A sudden silence fell on the Control Room. The 'Alert! Alert!' had ceased, but the Storm Tracker was still filled with thick, evil-looking purple smoke. It swirled and thickened and, even without the piercing alarm, it was the most menacing thing in the whole room.

"Projected location of the purple storm?" asked Captain Steadfast in a clipped, no-nonsense tone.

"The Standfirms' region," replied Brian, also speaking into a small tube, and looking closely at the Storm Tracker. He was examining the small, glass vials which were situated beneath the main Storm Tracker Indicator, attached to it by delicate metal pipes. There were fifteen clear vials. Each one represented a different part of Err. In one of them there was ominous, purple smoke similar to that which filled the main Storm Indicator Glass.

"Sir," said Bourne, stepping forward to Captain Steadfast's side, "we received a call from Satchel Standfirm about an hour ago. He feared a purple storm, rare though it is. He's due to call back with more details any moment now."

Captain Steadfast turned to one of the Rescuers who had accompanied him to the Central Control Room. "See that the call from Satchel Standfirm is patched through here, Jenny," he said.

Jenny vanished. Henrietta watched her leave wistfully. She wondered if she would ever wear the smart uniform the women Rescuers wore and have gold stripes on her shoulders. And even now Jenny was probably flying down the spiral staircase in the Gobbler, allowed to go wherever she wished in the Academy. Henrietta knew that they – the children – had momentarily been forgotten. She hoped they might escape the adults' notice long enough to hear and see everything about this intriguing purple storm. She hoped that Josie might stay quiet long enough to not spoil everything and get them all sent out of the room. But Josie was silently watching the activity going on around them; Dusty looked incapable of saying anything coherent, and Henrietta knew that Hugo wouldn't give them away: he would stay as quiet as possible and, like her, hope to go unnoticed.

"How long do we have until the storm hits, Brian?" asked Captain Steadfast.

"It's not showing on the Mission Detector or on the Weather Guide yet," said Brian, "so we should have upwards of uh, ten to twelve hours. We'll know more once it reaches our other radars."

"Naturally," said Captain Steadfast. "I want an estimate of how many Rescuers we have on the ground within ten hours reach of south-east Err where the Standfirms work."

"We'll have that to you in ten minutes," said Brian, dispatching a team of people in yellow coats, who all scattered to the Mission Detector machine.

"What do we estimate to be the centre of the Standfirms' territory?"

"Uh, that would be, uh…Idolatry," said Brian.

"Get me a Rescuer Transport estimate for a twenty mile radius of Idolatry," requested Captain Steadfast.

That was another task for the yellow coated team who managed the Mission Detector.

"Most importantly, what's our prayer power like for a large scale rescue mission in a purple storm?" asked Captain Steadfast.

Brian pointed at a man in a red coat who was already at work checking the individual prayer power sensors on the massive Prayer Power Monitor. He was looking at the reading on the small tube beneath the main dial which was labelled 'Standfirm'. Then he was checking various other screens and dials.

"Barely Adequate prayer power for the Standfirms," the red-coated man said grimly. "But we've got some good prayer coming through from the Run-the-Race Retirement Complex. And we can send a Red Priority message through to the Prayer Academy for targeted prayer for the mission…"

"Let's hope the purple storm doesn't clash with a good programme on Err-Vision," muttered Bourne to Harold. "That will really blow our prayer power!"

"Send the Red Priority message!" barked Captain Steadfast. "Barely Adequate prayer cover for the Standfirms indeed!" He looked appalled. "Get me Roger Stalwart of the Prayer Academy on the Mission Link," he ordered. "We need much more focussed prayer if we're even going to have a chance of a successful mission…"

"Satchel Standfirm is on the Mission Link now, sir," said the voice of Brian through the speaking tube.

There was a dubious crackling sound in the air around them. It wasn't clear where the voice of Satchel Standfirm was coming from, but they could hear his distant tones suddenly saying, "Hello? Hello? Is anybody there…?"

"Awesome!" said Dusty. But, to Henrietta's relief, none of the adults heeded Dusty.

"Ready Steadfast speaking," said Captain Steadfast. "You're patched through to the Central Control Room, Satchel. Go ahead and tell us all you can. How did you come to know about the purple storm in advance of our sensors?"

"...we...nothing certain...big occasion...Other-gods Conference Centre...creation...evil monster...death of... star..."

"You're breaking up, Satchel," said Captain Steadfast, "but I think we got some of it."

"I didn't!" Henrietta whispered to Hugo.

"Shhh...!" said Hugo back.

"...the death of a star that people idolised..."

"That'll be the football star that died!" exclaimed Dusty. "Lincoln Lionheart!"

He drew the startled gaze of Captain Steadfast who appeared to see him and the other children for the first time.

"...right..." came the crackling tones of Satchel Standfirm who had obviously heard Dusty. "...Lionheart..."

"And they're creating another god of this dead star, at the Other-gods Conference Centre?"

"Right," said Satchel more clearly this time. "There has been mass grief...hysteria...days. There will be...ceremony...new Lionheart god..."

"No wonder a purple storm is on the horizon!" muttered Bourne, and he actually shuddered.

Hugo and Henrietta exchanged glances. A purple storm was really that bad?

"Timescale, Satchel?" Captain Steadfast said urgently. "How long have we got before the ceremony and the purple storm hits?"

There was even worse crackling on the link than before. Everyone in the massive chamber held their breath and all the people in the coloured coats stopped to await Satchel Standfirm's response. But there was only more crackling and no voice at all.

"Satchel, if you can still hear me," said Captain Steadfast in firm tones, "we're preparing a Rescue Mission as we speak. You'll have everything we can spare, and we'll be on the ground at your Emergency Rendezvous as soon as we can be. We estimate ten to twelve hours before the storm hits, but we'll work to find out the timing of the new Lionheart-god ceremony and assume that will be when the purple storm is at its worst."

"To God, alone wise..." the faint tones of Satchel Standfirm were heard one last time.

"Be glory through Jesus Christ forever![15]" completed Captain Steadfast firmly.

And around the vast chamber all of the Rescuers, and all of the workers in coloured coats, shouted a great "Amen!"

CHAPTER 8
HENRIETTA'S PLAN

Following the excitement of the morning, the children's biggest fear was that they would be left out of the action surrounding the purple storm. Bourne and Harold were closeted in an important meeting with Captain Steadfast and other Rescuers. The children were given ham sandwiches and cookies and left in the Relaxation Room to have their lunch.

"I bet they think we'll just be in the way," said Hugo gloomily.

"I'd like to see the purple storm close up," said Dusty.

"I'd just like to go to Err," said Josie.

"I want to go on the rescue mission," said Henrietta.

They waited anxiously for the results of the emergency meeting. They quarrelled over exactly what a purple storm was (was it literally purple?), and tried to look up 'purple storm' on the Mission Detector which was in the Relaxation Room. But the Mission Detector kept blinking '*Unknown command*' and Hugo closed the lid on it in disgust.

When Bourne and Harold appeared in the doorway the children sat with bated breath.

"The kids don't seem very interested in the purple storm, Bourne," teased Harold.

"Perhaps we shouldn't take them with us after all," said Bourne.

It took a bewildered moment for his words to sink in and then Henrietta sprang from her chair and kissed both her brother and her cousin in incredulous delight.

"A purple storm is not a cause for celebration, Henry," Bourne remarked drily but with a twinkle in his eye.

"No, of course not," said Henrietta hastily.

"At least we get to go to Err," said Josie.

Dusty kept saying "Awesome!" as if he really meant it.

"You'll only really be staying in or close to the Rescue Capsule," said Harold. "Hugo, you'll be in charge of this group if Bourne and I have to move closer to the storm."

Hugo nodded. He was simply speechless. Not only were they getting a chance to go with real Rescuers into the land of Err as part of a massive rescue effort (even if they would only be used as an extra pair of hands to offload supplies), but they were actually travelling in a *Rescue Capsule*! He wondered if he was dreaming. At any moment he could wake up and none of this would be real...

"We leave in approximately three hours for the Standfirms' Emergency Rendezvous location," said Bourne. "Be ready for four o'clock *sharp*! Before then, we have a lot to do to get ready. We're carrying supplies in the Rescue Capsule to the Rendezvous. Most likely it'll just be a trip there and back, but you'll get to see some of Err from the air before it gets too dark and you will all be expected to help us unload the supplies. Hugo and Henry, you'll need to get kitted out with your armour."

Henrietta looked at her watch. It was past one o'clock in the afternoon. They were leaving at four o'clock. She had less than three hours. It was just enough time to carry out her plan.

Hugo, feeling very important, went to help Harold and Bourne load supplies onto the Rescue Capsule. Dusty, thinking that sleep was as good a preparation as any for the trip ahead, stretched out on one of the sofas in the Relaxation Room and snoozed. Josie cheered up when she found she could play around on the Mission Detector in the Relaxation Room. She began to look up all sorts of things she wanted to know about the part of Err – which she vaguely knew was on the banks of the River Self – to which they were flying. No one missed Henrietta when she slipped away.

Henrietta walked back down the corridor of the Academy and out of the main entrance. She knew the city of Aletheia well, and set off at once to jog across the pleasant green park behind the Academy to the Run-the-Race Retirement Home. It took her fifteen minutes to reach the Rest Home, and five more to find her way successfully through the corridors to the lounge where Mr Reuben Duffle often sat.

"I'm afraid he's having a bad day today," said the sympathetic nurse when Henrietta explained who she wanted and couldn't find. "Mr Duffle is confined to his bed."

"Oh," said Henrietta. "Is he allowed visitors?"

"Mostly he sleeps on his bad days," said the nurse. "I'm afraid he's too weak for visitors."

"Oh," said Henrietta again. "Does that mean that Mr Duffle isn't praying today?"

The nurse smiled. "I couldn't tell you that," she said. "If his mind is awake then likely he'll be praying, but he really is *very* weak."

Henrietta nodded slowly. It was a real blow to her plans. Perhaps that was why the Prayer Power dial in the Control Room was so low. Possibly it relied on old warriors like Mr Duffle praying. Whatever would happen when Mr Duffle was no longer on earth? Who was going to provide all the prayer power for the rescue missions?

Henrietta tried one more thing. "Did Mr Duffle leave any of his, uh…prayer sticks or other such things around?" she asked.

"Oh, I don't know, dear," said the nurse. "But I do know that they won't really help you unless he's been praying specifically for you."

"No," sighed Henrietta. "But he is so very good at prayer, isn't he?"

"I think Mr Duffle would say that it's not the power of the person praying that makes the difference, but the power of God," said the nurse. "Mr Duffle is the powerful prayer warrior that he is because he has absolute faith – that is confidence – in God. That's what makes the difference!"

"Right," said Henrietta. "Well…thanks very much for trying to help me…"

She glanced at her watch again. That was forty minutes gone.

She had set her watch for the four o'clock deadline. It was a useful watch and it now told her, '*Two hours, twenty minutes to departure. And don't forget you are twenty minutes from the Academy.*' It even added a smiley face because she was still in time. But she knew that if she was running late the smiley face would quickly turn to a scowling face to speed her on her way.

She must hurry. She had counted on enlisting Mr Duffle to pray for the rescue mission but she had failed. Now she had another stop she must make.

The Run-the-Race Retirement Home was just outside of the city centre of Aletheia. Beside it was the Prayer Academy, and, as Henrietta once more began to jog towards the city, she glanced at the towering Prayer Academy and hoped that somehow they had drummed up more prayer support for the mission. She cut through small, narrow city streets that she knew well, past her own home at the Foundation-of-Faith Apartments, and from there to the Fruit-of-the-Spirit shopping parade that she and Hugo had passed early that morning.

The shops in the parade were far livelier than they had been earlier. The Aletheians were busy about their business, making the most of the mild autumn day to get their shopping. Mr

Forbear had a queue going right outside of his Patience store. Henrietta could see people standing in line and craning their necks to where Mr Forbear appeared to be explaining something to Hilda Hasty, as if he had all the time in the world. She sped by Mr Forbear's door and slowed when she came to the Faithful store. Thankfully Mrs De Voté had a quiet spell and was quite alone. She looked up with interest as the little bell above her shop door tinkled and Henrietta entered.

"You look in quite a hurry, dear," she remarked. "It's Henrietta Wallop, isn't it? Have they got you running errands for the Academy all over Aletheia?"

"Well," Henrietta tried to catch her breath. "Not exactly," she said, "but I am sort-of on an important errand of my own!"

"How interesting," said Mrs De Voté. She put down the knitting she had in her hands. "You'll stay for tea, dear?" she asked. "I've got some fresh scones and…"

"Oh no, really I can't," said Henrietta, feeling awful for just rushing in and out of the shop. She vowed she would go back when there wasn't an emergency and help Mrs De Voté in her shop.

"Well," said the old lady, "what is it I can do for you, Henrietta?"

"I suppose it's really quite a cheek," began Henrietta. "I mean, I hardly know you, except passing by, and I've never really done anything for you, although I do look down at you and your shop sometimes from our balcony, but, you see, I'm rather desperate for some help."

Mrs De Voté was touched and amused. "I haven't had such an interesting customer for years," she mused, revealing a sense of humour that was largely unsuspected. "Well, out with it, Henrietta, for you look as if you're likely to rush away again at any moment!"

That was quite true. Henrietta had cast another glance of concern at her watch which was, thankfully, still smiling at her.

"It's about prayer," said Henrietta. "We need prayer!"

Mrs De Voté leaned forward on her chair behind the shop counter. "Do you?" she asked.

Henrietta was thankful that Mrs De Voté didn't laugh at her or doubt her.

"Something specific, is it?" asked Mrs De Voté.

"It's a purple storm," said Henrietta.

"Yes, I know it is," said Mrs De Voté.

"You do?"

Mrs De Voté nodded. "I'm on the Prayer Link," she said. "I received a Red Priority prayer request from the Prayer Academy not too long ago. A purple storm is a terrible thing."

"And…you'll pray?" asked Henrietta. She watched as Mrs De Voté picked up her knitting again and began rapid movements with her needles.

"Are you heading for the purple storm, Henrietta?" asked Mrs De Voté.

"Yes," said Henrietta. "We're going with a Rescue Capsule, with supplies. I don't suppose we'll be very near the storm." Suddenly she was not so sure that she wanted to be.

"Near enough," said Mrs De Voté. She finished clicking her needles and held up a square of blue knitting that Henrietta secretly thought looked a little tatty and unfinished. It had loose strands of wool hanging from the corners; it didn't look like anything special at all. "This is my pledge that I'll be praying for you," said Mrs De Voté.

Henrietta took the square of knitting, hoping she hid her doubtfulness at its appearance. "Thank you," she said. "I'll keep this safe!"

Mrs De Voté smiled. "It represents prayer," she said. "It doesn't need to be kept safe! It's intended to thwart the power of evil forces that would dare to question the true God!"

Henrietta turned to go.

"Remember, you must do your bit too, dear," said Mrs De Voté in parting. "I'll be praying for you, but you must do your bit too!" she repeated.

"Yes," said Henrietta. She wondered exactly what Mrs De Voté meant, but her watch had now lost its smile and there was an expression of some consternation on its face. Hurry, it seemed to say, hurry on...

"Go by Redemption Square, dear," Mrs De Voté said in parting. "Always go by the way of the cross!"

Henrietta took Mrs De Voté's advice and slipped through the narrow alleyway between buildings into Redemption Square. She had been there many times before. She knew it well. The square was a place of calm and quiet. It always had an atmosphere of something powerful and pure. In the middle of the large square, at the top of many steps, there was a plain cross. It marked the centre point of the city of Aletheia, and also the highest point. No building in Aletheia would ever rise higher. If you climbed the steps and stood close to the cross you could see the whole land of Err spread out around you in every direction. You could clearly see your way from that vantage point, and you could never be lost in the jumbled, crowded narrow city streets of Aletheia, because always you could look up and see the cross. Then you knew exactly where you were.

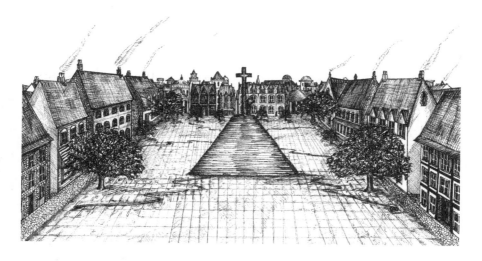

Henrietta took a moment to climb the many steps to the very foot of the cross. She knew that Mr and Mrs Standfirm worked as Outpost Rescuers in the south-east of Err: Captain Steadfast had said as much in the Control Room. She faced that direction and looked over the fields and forests and villages towards the rich, idolatrous towns that were part of the Standfirms' territory. In the far distance she could see an angry sky brewing. It was almost black, but there was a definite purple tinge about it, like a very ugly bruise. Even as she watched it was spreading, eating up the sky before it and heading into the land of Err.

"It's coming," she whispered to herself. "The purple storm is really coming!"

But the storm was small and insignificant from her place by the cross. Here, in the safety of its shadow, she was reminded of the great storm of judgement that the Lord Jesus had passed through when He died on the cross. He had endured great judgement and borne punishment so that she would never need to. He had taken her place when she trusted in Him. And now the Lord Jesus was the only safe refuge from the storm that was brewing in the land of Err.

CHAPTER 9
THE RESCUE CAPSULE

Henrietta didn't have any time to spare. She ran the last stretch to the Academy of Soldiers-of-the-Cross and plunged through the entrance, almost colliding with two young Rescuers.

"Steady!" one said with a smile.

Henrietta blushed. "Sorry!" she said.

One of the Contamination Detector screens winked at her as she passed through – at least, she was almost certain that it did actually wink – and she hurried down the corridor to the Relaxation Room where she had last seen the others. It felt good to know where she was going and what she was doing. She almost felt like a real Rescuer.

"At last!" said Hugo as his sister rushed through the doorway. "You look as if you've run a mile, Henry!"

"I think I have!" said Henrietta.

"I've got all your armour here," said Hugo. "I went to the armoury and got it in case we ran out of time."

"Armoury? Armour?" queried Dusty. He looked wonderfully

rested; in fact, he had slept most of the afternoon.

Josie had brushed her hair and looked neat and tidy. She had a large bag packed and ready to go. She shrugged at Dusty's query about armour. "They're just playing war games!" she said.

"You know quite well that's not true!" said Henrietta. "Even if you can't see it, you know that the armour of God is in the Bible!"

Josie shrugged again. She had the novel she was reading on her lap. She had been home and packed everything she might need in case of an 'emergency'. She looked as if she had been ready for hours.

"What armour do you mean?" pursued Dusty.

"We wear the armour of God[16] to keep us safe," said Hugo.

Dusty looked doubtful. "I can't see anything," he said, "except the Bible in that pouch at your side."

"That's the only thing people who aren't Christians can see of the armour," said Josie in a bored tone.

Henrietta looked indignant all over again.

"Leave it, Henry," Hugo said quietly. "She can't help herself."

Josie flushed an angry red but nobody took much notice. She had thought that she would at least have Dusty on her side. But he seemed inclined to be interested in everything and not necessarily to doubt it at all. Well, they would be sorry they had treated her like a child who would do whatever she was told. Soon they would eat all their words! Josie spent some moments imagining her cousin Henrietta in abject apology that she had got everything so wrong; in Josie's mind Hugo was saying "We should have listened to Josie all along"; and she could picture Dusty looking at her admiringly – partly because she was pretty, and partly because he, too, realised that she was right all along!

"Ready, Josie?" said Henrietta. "What *have* you got in that bag? We're only going for the evening, for an overnight if we're lucky, but we're not likely to see any action!"

Josie picked up her bag and followed the others from the room. "That's what you think," she muttered. "But just you wait and see!"

The Rescue Capsule restored the spirits of even Josie. It was difficult to be disdainful with such incredible surroundings. They had all seen Capsules of one sort or another skim over the sky, but none of them had ever been inside a fully equipped Rescue Capsule. Dusty was the only one of the four children who had once had a ride in a Capsule. The children of Topsy-Turvy had 'invested' the town's dwindling resources in one for the fun of it. But it had been broken within a year, and even when it was brand new it was nothing like the size and splendour of the Rescuers' flying machine.

"Capsule Three-Sixteen is a twelve-passenger Capsule," Hugo said proudly. He had helped to stock it with supplies for the mission and had already thoroughly explored the interior.

"We can all count twelve seats, Hugo," said Henrietta.

Hugo merely grinned. "That's at least two seats bigger than any other Capsule in Err!"

"Awesome!" said Dusty.

"Are you sure they don't have bigger Capsules in Celebrity?" said Josie.

Henrietta bit her tongue to keep from telling Josie to 'shut up'. She tried to fix her mind on what Harold had said to her earlier about Josie needing to be rescued. It was just difficult to help Josie when she was so incredibly annoying!

"Why are you looking at me like that, Henry?" asked Josie.

"It's just...oh, nothing," said Henrietta.

They all took their seats in the Capsule. Each seat was like a large armchair. As the Capsule was round, all of the seats faced inwards. So they were all sat facing each other across the Capsule, almost as if they were at a big round table. You could also swivel your chair around to the window to see the view, and, once the Capsule was flying, you could look through one of the peepholes on the floor of the Capsule and see the land beneath you. There was also one large skylight above them.

"The skylight takes in light and converts it to power," explained Hugo.

"Awesome!" said Dusty.

"It can use any light source for power," continued Hugo, glad of an appreciative audience. "Sunlight, moonlight, starlight, and if it's hit by lightning it can probably go to the moon and back!"

"Really?" said Josie.

Dusty laughed. "I don't think he means that!" he said.

The others laughed too and Josie swivelled her chair around and stared moodily out of the window. They were on the Launch Pad which was hidden at the top of one of the many towers of the Academy of Soldiers-of-the-Cross. There wasn't much to see from here. They were surrounded by an encircling stone wall that hid the Launch Pad and the Capsule and obscured the view. But Josie considered that it was still better than facing the others. The other three just laughed at her and thought she was stupid. Even Dusty. Well, she would show them in the end!

Harold and Bourne took their seats in the small pilots' compartment of the Capsule which was partitioned from the main cabin where the children sat, with a sound-proof screen in-between. Bourne sat in the first pilot's seat. There were a number of complex-looking dials and knobs and levers around them. Hugo longed for the day when he might be in that seat, in charge of a Rescue Capsule.

"Belts on, kids!" Bourne called through the speaking tube so they could hear him in the main cabin.

They fastened their seatbelts and Josie's chair automatically swivelled around to face the others again and clicked into place for take-off. There was a sudden, faint buzzing, like bumblebees feeding at distant flowers. They didn't feel the take-off. They were only aware of the smooth *click* of the long landing legs being tucked away neatly beneath the Capsule. Only when they looked through the peepholes on the floor did they realise they were no longer looking at the stones of the Launch Pad, but right over the city of Aletheia instead.

"I see our Foundation-of-Faith Apartments!" shouted

Henrietta. "There's the balcony...I'm sure that's Mum at the kitchen window!"

"I don't think so, Henry," said Hugo.

"Look, they've finished school for the day!" said Dusty.

They watched small groups of children, who looked about the size of ants, dispersing from the school.

"Aren't you glad we're here and not there!" exclaimed Hugo.

"Awesomely glad!" agreed Dusty.

"I think the Academy of Rescuers looks like the biggest thing in Aletheia," said Henrietta.

"And the Prayer Academy is the highest," said Hugo.

"Apart from the cross."

"Apart from the cross," agreed Hugo.

"What do you like best, Josie?" asked Henrietta.

The chairs had been freed from their take-off position and Josie had swivelled her armchair to look out of her own round window. At Henrietta's question she swivelled back around to face the others. "Why are you asking me?" she said suspiciously.

Henrietta sighed. Even trying to be nice to Josie ended up being an annoying experience. "Forget it," she said.

Quickly, so quickly, the Capsule rose high above the city of Aletheia. Very soon they could see the entire city beneath them, with the surrounding Pray-Always farms dotted like tiny, accidental splashes across the patchwork fields, and the deep flowing Water of Sound Doctrine surrounding it all.

"I've always wondered why Aletheia didn't just build a city wall," said Dusty, "instead of all that water, you know?"

"Dad says the water is the best defence the city could have," said Hugo.

"How?" asked Dusty. "People can swim you know, or they could build loads of bridges and come into the city and even take over."

"I don't see why anyone would want to," muttered Josie. She was staring out of her window again as if she didn't want to see the others at all.

"Oh, people would want to live in Aletheia alright," said Dusty cheerfully. "It's much nicer than the towns in Err that I've seen, but they might not want the religion, and stuff about the Bible, see? So they might just want to move into the city and get rid of all the Bible stuff..." he trailed off uncertainly. He really didn't want to offend Hugo and Henrietta.

"Well, I've never seen this myself," said Hugo, "but I've heard that people fear to cross the Water of Sound Doctrine; and the four bridges across the water into Aletheia can be raised at any moment, you know."

"Why would people fear the water?" asked Dusty, clearly intrigued at the idea.

"Because the Water of Sound Doctrine shows you as you are," said Hugo.

"I hope not," said Dusty, "because it's always looked pretty dirty and muddy and cloudy to me! And yet you drink it!" he added wonderingly.

"I suppose people would see awful things in the water if they attempted to takeover Aletheia," said Hugo reflectively. "I suppose they might see monsters and even horrible dead and decaying things in the water!"

"You don't know that," said Josie.

"You don't know…!" began Henrietta, but she bit her lip and stopped. It was an awful thing that Josie didn't like the Water of Sound Doctrine. Josie had drunk it since she was a small child, until it no longer suited her taste. Now Josie, along with the other children in Aletheia that weren't Christians, drank bottled water instead. It just showed how badly she needed to be rescued.

"I see it!" Dusty suddenly cried. He released his seat belt and darted across the Capsule to peer out of the window. Hugo and Henrietta quickly followed Dusty and looked where he was pointing.

"The purple storm!" cried Dusty. "I see the purple storm!"

CHAPTER 10
A WILD RIDE

The purple storm hadn't grown much in size since Henrietta had first seen it from the foot of the cross. It still looked like an angry black and purple bruise glowering at them from the horizon.

"It's small," said Dusty.

"It looks fierce," said Hugo.

"It's like a dog on a chain," said Henrietta. "It wants to gobble us right up, but it can't seem to get free!"

Dusty laughed.

"It's nothing much," muttered Josie. She had grown quieter and more moody as the flight progressed. The others heard her but ignored her. The view from the windows was fascinating and there was no time to pay any attention to Josie. Soon they got used to the purple storm hanging in the distance and spent their time spotting people and vehicles and animals on the ground below. Now and again they saw the glint of gold flying past the window of the Capsule. It wasn't unusual to see money and gold flying around the skies of Err instead of being in people's pockets and banks. All of the children who were brought up in Err and Aletheia quickly learned that if you loved money too much, it would grow wings and fly away[17].

Bourne saved precious energy in the Capsule by flying in wind currents for the first part of their flight. He had flown north and skimmed over Tragedy, which was, as usual, obscured by a thick grey cloud. Tragedy was one of the most isolated towns in Err despite being quite close to Aletheia. It was such a depressing place that only stalwart Rescuers and Mrs Payne Hope, who was the resident Outpost Rescuer, visited the people there. The children hadn't observed the town. They had taken no notice of whatever might be beneath such a gloomy cloud. They had flown close to the town of Resentment which was hidden behind thick, dark trees; really Resentment just looked like a seething, impenetrable forest. Now Bourne was flying the Capsule south east. They flew over the majestic town of Pride, which was a constantly expanding town of the most unashamed, shiny tidiness. Pride had won the 'Err in Bloom' competition for the last ten years. Josie thought it might be a nice town to visit, although in reality it was an extremely irritating place. Everybody just wanted to talk about themselves. Anybody who lived there had no time to listen to stories about anyone else. Conversations consisted of everyone talking at once and nobody listening.

Now, ahead of the flying Capsule, a raging river snaked through the land of Err like a long, ugly, unhealed cut.

"Look down there!" cried Dusty. "Look at that town where the river has burst its banks!"

Harold had come back into the main cabin to join the children. "That's Muddled-by-Self," he explained.

"It must be pretty *muddy* there anyway!" said Hugo.

"Was that meant to be a joke?" asked Henrietta.

"Actually," said Harold, "there is a story that the people who first settled in Muddled-by-Self intended to call the town 'Muddied-by-Self', because the River Self was always bursting its banks and causing mud there."

"Ha, ha!" laughed Dusty.

"But somebody got uh…*muddled* when they wrote the sign for the town, and so they called the town 'Muddled-by-Self'!"

The two boys laughed loudly.

"That's not really a very good joke," said Henrietta.

"But it is a pretty accurate description of the town," said Harold. "Because that's exactly what the people there are like.

They are muddled by themselves."

"Muddled by themselves?" asked Dusty.

"The people in Muddled-by-Self believe they have the answer to everything in life themselves and don't need any other help to find it," said Harold. "They don't acknowledge God in their lives; instead they talk endlessly of their own version of what is good and true and right, and only end up unhappy and disillusioned and hopelessly muddled."

Dusty stared at the untidy, desolate town retreating into the distance. That was exactly

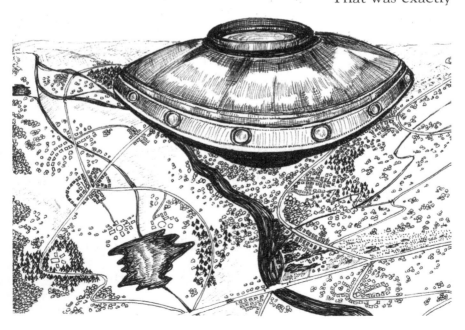

what he believed! Dusty thought he could figure out everything himself and find all the answers to happy, peaceful living somewhere in Err. And yet – people that believed what he did were living in a small, grubby town that was constantly flooded by the raging River Self.

"Why would people build a town where the River Self bursts its banks?" asked Henrietta.

"The River Self is always too full," said Harold. "It's always overflowing and it always will be while people are so full of themselves. Look at it raging just now! I don't know how high it might get with this purple storm coming!"

"They should move further back, away from the river," said Dusty.

"They can't," said Harold. "The pull of the Self is too strong."

Dusty wondered what he meant, but Harold left the children and returned to the co-pilot's seat.

The flight now followed the course of the River Self. Beneath them, through the peepholes in the floor, the children could see a landscape of largely trees and bogs and winding roads. They were passing over Compromise and close to Alternative Teaching. Hugo and Henrietta looked closely at the small streets of Alternative Teaching and the dots of houses and shops. They had been to Alternative Teaching once before, on their adventure in the land of Err in the summer. But they were flying too high and too fast to make out Dough's tumble-down café where they had discovered the foul Black Beetle Beverage.

"The storm has moved!" Dusty exclaimed suddenly.

They stopped peering through the peepholes in the floor of the Capsule and gathered around Dusty at the window. Even Josie came, unable to resist the growing excitement.

"The storm is hanging in the air," said Hugo.

"Awesome!" said Dusty.

"It doesn't exactly seem like a storm," said Josie.

"How strange it looks!" exclaimed Henrietta.

"You would look pretty strange if you were hovering around like that," observed Hugo.

"But even for clouds, even for weather, it looks downright weird!" said Henrietta.

The others agreed. There was something alien about the menacing black and purple clouds that were boldly claiming the sky. It was as if they were poised to dump their evil purple load on the hapless Other-gods Conference Centre above which the centre of the storm now hung.

"I wonder when it moved," said Dusty. "One minute it was brewing over there..." he waved his hand vaguely in the direction of the south-east of Err, "and the next moment it was suddenly there!" And 'there' was very definitely the small cluster of buildings and the big lake that formed the Other-gods Conference Centre.

Suddenly, without any warning, the Capsule dropped from the sky. Like a stone it fell, sending the children shooting upwards towards the ceiling, before they fell back down with a *bump* onto the floor.

"Seatbelts fastened!" Bourne's voice boomed into the cabin.

"It would be something if we could even get into our seats!" exclaimed Hugo, struggling to stand as the Capsule suddenly shot violently sideways.

"We're going to hit the trees!" shrieked Josie.

"We really are just about at tree height!" exclaimed Henrietta. Both girls were still sprawled on the floor and clutching at the small rims of the peepholes there. And they were looking directly into the branches of trees.

Hugo hauled Josie by her ankle and managed to get her to a chair.

"Hold on!" came Harold's urgent voice through the loudspeaker tube.

Which was precisely what the children could not do. Not one of them had their seatbelts fastened, and suddenly the Rescue Capsule catapulted straight up into the air. They were in a strange purple-tinged funnel which seemed determined to spew the entire Capsule high into space! And then suddenly they were released from the strange funnel and they were flying again, with Bourne and Harold swiftly regaining control.

Henrietta's stomach was churning from the sudden turbulence and fright, and all of the others looked pretty sick. Dusty had a big bump on his head, and Hugo was clutching his arm as if he had hurt it.

"Grab a seat!" urged Hugo, "it might happen again!"

This time they all managed to reach a seat and fasten their seatbelts. They stared across the cabin at each other, too shocked to speak.

"What happened?" asked Hugo.

"Air pockets?" suggested Dusty faintly.

"Some air pocket!" said Henrietta.

"It was purple!" said Josie in wonder.

"Is everyone alright back there?" came Harold's voice.

Hugo detached a speaking tube from the arm of his chair. "We're Ok," said Hugo. "What was it?"

"The outskirts of the purple storm," said Harold.

"The *outskirts* of the storm?" echoed Henrietta. "What must it be like in the centre?!"

"Stay in your seats, we don't know when it might hit again," warned Harold.

"It's funny, we can't even see any of the storm yet, but it's still throwing us around!" said Josie.

"There's not much funny about this storm," said Dusty. He looked pale and shaken.

"But there's no purple here…" But as Josie spoke a tiny burst of purple smoke gave one little puff in the middle of the Capsule, and then it vanished.

"Did you see…?"

"Was that real?"

"What on earth…?"

"Hugo!" exclaimed Henrietta. "Did you just make a bad smell?"

"No, I jolly well did not!" said Hugo indignantly.

But there was certainly an extremely unpleasant smell around them. It was something like the smell of rotten eggs.

"Well, don't look at me!" said Josie. "I certainly didn't…!"

"I think it was the purple smoke thing," said Dusty.

"There it is again!" said Henrietta. "Oh! It's gone again!"

Another tiny burst of strange, malignant, purple smoke was there one moment, and the next it had utterly vanished away.

"Uh…" Harold's voice came once more into the main cabin over the speaking tube. "Sorry kids," he said, "but we're having some problems with our protective filters. Hugo and Henry, put on your helmets of salvation. The purple smoke isn't poisonous, but it will begin to affect your mind…"

Neither of the twins could reach their helmet of salvation from their chair. Everything had been jostled about during the violent turbulence they had been through, and now there were bits and pieces all over the floor.

"We should have worn it all along," said Henrietta in a subdued sort of voice. She knew that the helmet of salvation[16] would keep her mind on what the Lord Jesus had done for her and how He had defeated everything that was evil at the cross.

Wearing the helmet of salvation would also help her to be patient with Josie: because it would remind Henrietta that the Lord Jesus had died for Josie too – if she would only accept what He had done and trust in Him.

"What about me and Josie?" asked Dusty in a troubled voice. "We don't have helmets of salvation to protect us!"

"It's nothing," muttered Josie. "Don't worry about it."

"It's everything!" said Henrietta, trying to see her helmet through the jumble of things on the floor of the Capsule.

After a while they got used to the sight of tiny puffs of purple smoke appearing and vanishing in unexpected corners of the Capsule. The vile smell of something like rotten eggs became more constant and Dusty commented that it wouldn't matter if someone made a bad smell now, because nobody would notice.

"That's disgusting!" said Josie.

"Yuk!" said Henrietta.

But then they forgot all about the purple smoke and the bad smell. For once again the Capsule plunged violently downwards, then sideways, then straight up in the air. Then it was spinning wildly around in a circle, round and round, faster and faster, until they were convinced that their heads would spin off their shoulders and land in the jumble of things that were strewn across the floor. It was a far more wild and terrifying experience than the ride on the Gobbler at the Academy of Soldiers-of-the-Cross. All of the children knew that something completely unexpected had happened, something to do with the storm. And now the Capsule might be anywhere: they might have been flung straight into the middle of the purple storm itself!

Suddenly, from the pilots' compartment, they heard an alarm sound.

"Not another alarm!" groaned Henrietta, trying to be light-hearted about it.

But her voice shook and the others looked as white and scared as she did. The alarm was harsh and urgent, the type of alarm that just sounded as if it meant disaster.

From the little they could see of Harold and Bourne there was some frantic activity as they pulled levers and turned dials and pushed buttons. But the alarm only got louder and more insistent.

"We're going to crash!" shrieked Josie. "We're all going to die!"

CHAPTER 11
EMERGENCY LANDING!

"Alright, kids?" Harold's voice came calmly through the speaking tube.

"We're fine," said Hugo stoically.

"Are we going to die?" cried Josie.

"Of course not!" snapped Henrietta. "I expect we'll just have to throw you out of the Capsule to lighten the load and get airborne again!"

It wasn't a helpful comment and Josie's wail was her response.

"Sorry," muttered Henrietta. It was pretty easy to feel annoyed with Josie at the best of times. And right now Henrietta felt as sick as a dog with all the wild swoops and swirls the Capsule had been making, and scared to death with the sound of that awful alarm that Bourne and Harold had somehow silenced. But it was certainly true that they needed to get airborne again, because the Capsule was flying very low indeed. No longer was it thrown about the sky, it flew smoothly once more, although there was a definite hesitation in it, as if it was reluctant to fly.

"Stay seated," Harold instructed from the pilots' compartment. "We think we're out of the purple funnels, but we can't be sure."

"Can you see our helmets, Hugo?" asked Henrietta.

"Afraid not, old thing," said Hugo. "Just when we need them too!"

"Purple funnels don't sound too good," said Henrietta.

"I've never heard of them," said Dusty.

"It must be part of the storm," said Josie.

Henrietta bit back a sharp retort that that was obvious.

"Are we going to land, Harold?" asked Hugo through the speaking tube.

"Sit tight," said Harold.

"It's not like we've got much choice," muttered Josie.

"We're going to talk to the Central Control Room at the Academy," said Harold. "You'll hear the conversation because our communications system is somewhat, uh, damaged. But please don't interrupt!"

Hugo knew that Bourne and Harold would have isolated the call to the Control Room if they could. He was very glad they would get to hear whatever was going on.

"Let's hope that Brian really knows what he's doing in the Control Room," murmured Hugo. "I didn't think he looked that switched-on when we saw him earlier."

"Perhaps the orange cardigan put you off," said Henrietta.

"I don't think that's very kind," said Josie.

"It was just a comment about a cardigan!" retorted Henrietta.

"I can nearly see birds' nests in the trees," said Dusty. "I wouldn't want to fly much lower!"

"Soon you won't be able to see the trees," said Josie. "It's almost dark."

It was true. The afternoon was later than they supposed, the view from all of the windows was now growing dim and the grey clouds had a definite purple-ish hue.

There was loud crackling and popping in the air around them.

"Shhh!" said Hugo. "Let's hear what the Control Room…"

"Capsule Three-Sixteen, Capsule Three-Sixteen, come in, we now have a link with you…this is Mr Brian Buffer, Central Control Room Manager speaking," came a hollow voice.

"We have lost power input," said Bourne crisply and calmly. "Currently running on stored reserves."

"Do you know your approximate hours of stored reserves?" queried the voice.

"Estimate two hours; repeat, two hours."

"Received," said Brian.

"He doesn't sound particularly concerned!" hissed Henrietta.

"Location uncertain," said Bourne. "The onboard Mission Detector is somewhat, uh, slow. We think the purple pollution is affecting it."

"Checking your location," said Brian.

"Go Brian!" said Hugo.

Henrietta smothered a giggle, surprised she could laugh in this crisis.

"We had, uh, intermittent sightings of you for a while there, Lieutenant" said Brian. "We lost you from our screens entirely on occasions."

"We've been caught in turbulence and currents from the storm," said Bourne. "Visibility now very limited and onboard Mission Detector system still not showing our current location."

"Checking location and sending intel to your onboard Detector," said Brian. "Ah, yes, we have you...Alternative Teaching two miles north, low flying altitude..."

"You can say that again!" murmured Dusty. "I'm sure we almost hit a branch!"

"Good," said Bourne. "We're not as far off course as I feared. Where is the nearest light source for power refuel?"

"Nearest unpolluted light power source, uh, Apathy, approximately twenty miles west-north-west."

"Too far," muttered Harold.

"Good job we conserved power earlier in the flight," responded Bourne.

"Uh, Lieutenant Faithful, Capsule Three-Sixteen is equipped to use Water of Sound Doctrine as an alternative fuel source in emergencies," said Brian. "In, uh, theory anyway."

"Clarify," said Bourne. "Has this been tested?"

"Uh, no, Lieutenant. Transport Lab has, uh, yet to confirm the, uh, findings of that experiment, but it might be worth trying if necessary."

"Noted," said Bourne.

"Someone really needs to light a fire under that Transport Lab," muttered Harold.

In silence Hugo and Henrietta looked gleefully at one another. It was fun listening into the adults' conversation when they knew quite well they had been forgotten.

"Is the cause of power source failure known?" asked Bourne.

There was some crackling over the airwaves and the children could hear the voice of Brian Buffer of the orange cardigan speaking to someone in the background. "Well, get onto it then, Jim," he was saying. "They need to know *now*!"

Henrietta giggled and even Josie was amused.

"Poor Jim," said Hugo.

"Uh...poor Jim?" echoed Brian uncertainly.

"They heard!" whispered Henrietta. "They can hear us!" And all of the children smothered the hysterical laughter that threatened to overwhelm them even at this most critical juncture.

"Source of power failure?" Bourne repeated sternly and the children immediately subsided into sobriety.

"Uh, yes, coming now...I'm afraid the source of light power failure is unknown," said Brian, sounding most perturbed.

"I bet Jim's in trouble!" Hugo couldn't resist whispering.

"Our nearest estimate is that it's caused by pollution from the purple storm," said Brian.

"Way to go, Brian!" Hugo whispered, "I think we could have guessed that!"

"Purple storms are, uh, relatively infrequent, with, uh, very unpredictable behaviour patterns, and our, uh, data is limited." Brian sounded very apologetic. Henrietta began to feel sorry for Jim and for Brian too. There seemed to be so many things about the land of Err that even a complex room full of very clever people and marvellous machines couldn't figure out. "We're working on coordinates for the nearest safe landing place," said Brian.

"As close as you can get us to the River Self crossing," requested Bourne.

"Noted. Uh…stand by for coordinates…"

"Standing by," said Bourne. He was still very calm, but there was an edge to his voice. He must land Capsule Three-Sixteen away from the Emergency Rendezvous agreed upon, in the land of Err, on the edge of a massive, unpredictable purple storm, with four children who were never meant to be included in such a plan. Hugo was fervently thankful that Harold and Bourne and the other Rescuers had never anticipated that things might go so wrong; they would never have been able to come on such an adventure if they had!

"Uh, Lieutenant, here are your landing coordinates. Seventeen north, nineteen north-west, three point nine-eight miles, altitude one hundred feet minimum; repeat, one hundred feet minimum."

"Thanks," said Bourne briefly.

"Landing space screened by trees, uh, only half a mile from the town of Alternative Teaching."

"Right," said Bourne.

"Uh, Lieutenant, remember unpredictable wind pattern; we're unable to predict wind direction on landing."

"Aware of that," said Bourne tersely.

"Aren't we all!" said Dusty.

There was tense silence in the Capsule as the call with Brian at the Control Room ended and Bourne and Harold began to press buttons and pull levers and turn the limping Capsule towards the identified landing space. There was a time, at the start of the flight, when the children could not imagine ever wanting to leave the marvel that was Capsule Three-Sixteen. But now, with the constant smell of rotten eggs, the frequent malevolent puffs of purple smoke, and the unpredictable swirling and swooping of the Capsule, they would be fervently thankful to stand on solid ground again and breathe fresh air.

Slowly the Capsule headed for the landing space. Beneath them, through the purple darkness, the children could detect the stark, grabbing branches of tall trees. Bourne switched on landing lights, and then they could see a flat clearing in the middle of the trees, just big enough to take the large Capsule, but not big enough for any mistakes.

They barely dared to move as the Capsule began to circle lower into the landing space. One puff of the malicious wind of the purple storm and Capsule Three-Sixteen would be no more.

Henrietta thought about the blue square of knitting that was in her pocket. She hoped Mrs De Voté was praying. Henrietta closed her eyes  and prayed.

CHAPTER 12
LEFT BEHIND

There was an unhealthy *crunch* when Three-Sixteen touched the ground. The Capsule was no longer level: instead it sloped drastically downwards on one side. Two of the four long landing legs had been damaged in the turbulence and it stuck up on one side like a broken toy. All of the stuff that had come loose on the wild flight tumbled to the lowest side of the Capsule; the Rescuers' supplies had thankfully been secured by Bourne and Harold, and their ropes and knots held the big crates in place.

"Otherwise..." said Henrietta cheerfully as they began to disentangle themselves from their seatbelts, "otherwise we might have been squashed to death!"

"I don't think that's very funny," said Josie.

"It wouldn't have been funny at all!" agreed Henrietta. Josie's seat was at the lowest point of the diagonal slope and much of the children's bags and bits and pieces were strewn around and on top of her. "You would have been well and truly pulped if the supplies had come loose!" said Henrietta.

There was such a feeling of relief amongst them, now that

they were safely on the ground again, that the danger of the storm, and the damaged Rescue Capsule, and the power loss, and whatever else, seemed somehow surreal.

Bourne and Harold clambered from the slanting pilots' cabin and one by one the children and the Rescuers extracted themselves and stood on the damp, green grass that was long and lush in the clearing in the middle of the trees. The light was very dim, but Bourne turned on the Capsule's outside lights which shone brightly around the clearing. Bourne and Harold examined the underside of the damaged Capsule. They spoke quietly together, obviously working out a plan which they did not want the children to overhear. The four children wandered around the clearing. It was still and sheltered, and, had it not been for the lingering odour of rotten eggs in the air, the children might have imagined they had dreamt up the purple

storm entirely. But there was no escaping the scent of the storm, and here and there, when they least expected it, they could see a tiny purple puff exuding that awful smell.

Harold and Bourne decided to retract the two long landing legs that were working and the Capsule at last lay flat against the ground. They all clambered back into the main cabin and tidied up the bits and pieces that lay around. Then they each took a seat in the big armchairs that faced each other across the cabin: a solemn assembly of two grim faced Rescuers and four children who were wondering what would happen next.

"It's imperative that Harold and I get to the Emergency Rendezvous on the other side of the River Self," said Bourne. "Unfortunately we can't risk taking you with us, so, Hugo, that leaves you in charge of the others and you all remaining here. Do you think you can manage?"

"Yes," said Hugo.

"I don't see why…" began Josie.

"We're relying on you all to help us out here," said Bourne. "We didn't anticipate leaving you, but the most important thing you can do to help us is to stay put here and stick together. I'm afraid you'll be here for the night; we'll hopefully be back with you by the morning. Stay in the Capsule as much as possible. Only go outside if you need to. Don't go far. Remember the storm isn't at its full strength yet and it may get a lot wilder even on the outskirts. On *no account* attempt to cross the River Self!"

Hugo looked sober with importance and listened attentively to every word; Henrietta looked slightly disappointed that they were to remain so hidden away from the action; Dusty looked subdued and ready to obey; it was hard to tell what Josie was thinking.

"Do you hear me, Josie?" asked Bourne.

"Of course I can hear you," she said.

"I'm afraid you must try and conserve energy while we're gone," said Harold. "Only use the Capsule's lights as necessary, and get to sleep early. You'll find the armchairs recline and are very comfortable. You can use your Bibles for light if you need to." This was because the Bible, the Word of God, shone as a real light[18] in the land of Err. For those who believed, it always showed sufficient light for whatever needed to be done.

"Any questions?" asked Bourne.

"Can we use the Mission Detector?" asked Hugo.

"Because of the power shortage, please limit use to emergencies only," said Bourne. "If you're really stuck you can call Brian at the Control Room, but only in an emergency. I'll show you how to do this before we go, Hugo. Anything else?"

"Uh, will you both be alright?" asked Henrietta.

"With sufficient prayer cover we'll have the protection we need, in the will of God," said Bourne.

"*Is* there sufficient prayer cover?" asked Dusty interestedly.

"We'll soon find out," murmured Harold.

"What exactly is in the storm?" asked Dusty. "I mean, it's not rain and thunder, is it? It's weird smoke and bad smells and stuff."

"The storm is the accumulation of evil and confusion that has come about because people are rejecting the God of the Bible and choosing to trust in someone or something else instead," explained Bourne. "This purple storm has come because tonight people are gathering to celebrate this new god they have invented, the dead football star, Lincoln Lionheart. It's a very serious thing to turn from the one, true God and the only way of salvation and trust in someone else instead."

"I think if I was the real God I would knock them all down dead!" said Dusty. "Why doesn't God just do that?"

"Because today God is dealing with people in love and

forgiveness – which the Bible calls grace.[19]"

"What's grace?" asked Dusty.

"Grace describes the way that God offers love and mercy and forgiveness to those who don't deserve it. Grace is why the Lord Jesus came to earth to die so that people who trust in Him can be saved. All of the people who trust in other things instead of in God, everyone who will attend the celebration of their idol Lincoln Lionheart, anyone and everyone, no matter what they have done, can still turn to God and ask for forgiveness. That is because God is dealing with people in grace and offers forgiveness when we don't deserve it at all. That's why He doesn't act in judgement just now."

"So, it's because of grace that God offers forgiveness when we don't deserve it, and we have to accept His offer by faith?" said Dusty.

"Exactly right!" said Bourne. "The Bible says, that you are saved by grace, through faith.[20]"

"Remember what we said about faith?" asked Harold.

"I think so," said Dusty. "Faith is trusting in everything the Bible says about God even though we can't see Him."

"Yes," said Harold. "Faith is resting on God, that what He says is true."

"People generally have faith in something, even if it's only in themselves and their own ability to find peace and happiness," said Bourne. "That is faith without substance. It's believing in things that won't really help you at all."

Dusty thought of the people of Muddled-by-Self. He didn't think that he was really like them, living in mud and confusion. But he was certainly trusting in himself to find the way to live a peaceful and happy life somewhere outside of Topsy-Turvy. Could he really and truly trust in himself to find the answers? Or did he need Someone far greater? Did he need God?

"You must be very sure that your faith – your confidence – is placed in someone who is worthy of your trust and who will never let you down," said Bourne. "Christians believe that the only One who can be absolutely trusted is God. Faith must always have some promise of God as its foundation. That's why the Bible is so important: because it is the Word of God[21] and contains all God's promises."

The darkness was increasing outside the Capsule as Bourne and Harold hefted their heavy rucksacks onto their backs. Soon the children would be left alone with only the damaged Capsule to protect them from the storm.

"Often in a purple storm the false things that people believe are seen as real creatures," Bourne warned them in parting. "If you see and hear the creatures of the storm you mustn't place your trust in them. Trust only in what the Bible says about the one, true God[22]. Remember what the Bible promises about God's character – that He is faithful, and just[13], and a God of grace, and love, and forgiveness. God alone is our refuge and strength in the storm![23]"

It was still calm in the forest clearing when Bourne and Harold departed. There were only a few of the foul smelling purple puffs in the air around them. But somewhere beyond their shelter at the Capsule the children knew that the purple storm was threatening.

"I don't know why you kept asking those questions about faith and stuff," said Josie when Bourne and Harold had vanished into the trees.

"Because I want to know," said Dusty.

"I thought you didn't believe in the Bible," said Josie. "I thought you were going to explore the land of Err and try other things and not just believe in God."

Dusty shrugged. He didn't particularly want to upset Josie, who was looking pretty moody.

Josie was rummaging in her large bag on the floor of the Capsule. "Can someone put the light on?" she demanded.

"We're conserving energy," said Hugo. "You heard what Harold and Bourne said about that..."

"Fine!" snapped Josie. "Have it your way!"

"It's not exactly my way," said Hugo, as peaceably as possible.

"What's got into you?" exclaimed Henrietta. "You're biting his head off, and actually you look pretty sick too!"

"Sick yourself!" retorted Josie. She fastened her bag and hoisted it up onto her back.

"She looks sort of...purple tinged," said Dusty.

"Shut up," said Josie. "Just because you're getting into Bible stuff and you're on *their* side!"

Dusty did shut up. He didn't understand girls at the best of times and Josie was one of the more puzzling specimens, especially right now.

"Where are you going, Josie?" asked Hugo. He was beginning to wonder if being 'in charge' was really going to be as much fun as he had imagined it would be. Did Bourne and Harold know what it was like to be in charge of girls, especially one as difficult as Josie? And, unbelievable as it might seem, Josie really did look...*purple tinged*. Neither Harold nor Bourne had said anything about the children becoming coloured with the storm!

"I'm going to explore," said Josie.

"You can't go out!" exclaimed Hugo. "Really you can't, Josie, there's the storm, and..."

"Storm of your granny!" retorted Josie. "There's no storm right here, look!"

She flung open the Capsule door. There was stillness in the forest clearing. No wind, no rain, no purple in sight if you discounted the short, sharp purple puffs that vanished almost before you had seen them.

"Honestly, Josie..." Hugo began to remonstrate.

"Are you coming?" demanded Josie. "I'm only going into Alternative Teaching which is just through the trees. Then we can come back again for the night."

"But Bourne said..." said Hugo.

"I'll come," said Dusty. "I mean, I think we should do what Bourne and Harold said, but I don't suppose there's much harm in going into the local town and back. It looked like a pretty decent place from above, everything the right way up!"

"It's only in Topsy-Turvy that things are the wrong way up!" said Josie. She was encouraged by Dusty's response. At last someone might be on her side.

"I really think…" began Hugo desperately.

"We'd better go with them if they're going, Hugo," said Henrietta. "We're the only ones with armour, and they might need our help!"

Poor Hugo looked helplessly around at the others. He had no intention of disobeying Bourne's orders. But if they were going away from the safety of the Capsule and into Alternative Teaching, then his place, as their leader, was with them: making sure they returned safely.

"I think it's affecting her mind," he whispered desperately to Henrietta as they followed the other two into the clearing and began to pick their way through the trees.

"What is?" said Henrietta. "Whose mind?"

"Josie's mind! The purple smoke is affecting her mind!"

Henrietta looked anxiously ahead to where her cousin walked with Dusty. Josie was happy now, confident, swaggering. Josie might always be a rebel, but she was not usually courageous. She was generally scared of the dark. And yet here she was, walking through a strange forest, heading to an unknown town, on the outskirts of a terrifying purple storm.

Something strange was surely at work; something very strange.

CHAPTER 13
THE RIVER SELF

They followed Josie through the trees that surrounded the safely hidden Rescue Capsule. They had no notion whether the direction in which they were heading was the right direction for the town of Alternative Teaching: Josie had simply taken the route that Bourne and Harold had taken earlier. But there was no light of a town or houses or shops through the trees. Instead, very soon, they heard the roar of the raging River Self.

There was something strangely compelling, but quite terrifying, about the monstrous river. Waves of water surged and broke on one another as the churning, boiling, angry mass rushed headlong through the land of Err, cutting through the earth like a large, ugly, weeping sore. From the foaming torrent strange purple tendrils of smoke or spray – it was not clear which – rose and fell. It was almost as if they were waving hands, beckoning the watching children to come. Over the whole river was a vague purple mist. It hung in the air, not living and moving, but seeming sinister and malicious nonetheless.

"I think we should go back," said Hugo.

"It's not safe," said Henrietta.

"It's just water," said Josie.

"It's like…it's like it's calling us," said Dusty, wide-eyed.

"Didn't Harold say something about the pull of the River Self when we were talking about the people of Muddled-by-Self?" said Henrietta.

Ahead of them, beyond the river, the land of Err was dim and unclear. The twilight, which was now nearly the darkness of night, had a definite purple hue. Through it they could faintly make out the shape of trees, perhaps rocks, maybe a path or a road. But the shapes changed and shifted uneasily and it was not clear what lay beyond. A cold, foul smelling wind wafted the purple darkness towards them.

Closer to them, at the very edge of the mighty torrent, waves lapped hungrily at the banks, sucking and gurgling. It was as if the River Self desired the children to take the plunge into the midst of the surging water. Josie stood still and watchful with a strange expression on her face. Hugo was afraid the river might take her away; it almost seemed as if she belonged to the Self.

"We're going to Alternative Teaching, remember?" urged Hugo. He never imagined he would feel so compelled to lead them to a town in Err but suddenly the town of Alternative Teaching seemed mundane and safe after standing at the banks of the River Self. It was too greedy, too uncontrolled, too terrifying in its raging.

"Do you see yourself?" asked Josie. "Do you see what the river shows you?"

"Shows you?" faltered Hugo, fearing that Josie's mind was becoming unhinged with the effect of the purple pollution.

"I'm beautiful," said Josie. "Do you see?"

Henrietta was about to retort that it was nothing new that her cousin considered herself beautiful when she, too, peered into the currents of water, following Josie's gaze.

"It makes you…" Henrietta stared at her own reflection, which seemed oddly unaffected by the surging waves and currents of the fast moving water. Her reflection didn't move at all. Her face was looking back at her, as clear as a mirror. "…it can't be…" Henrietta said faintly. In the reflected version of her she wasn't wearing her helmet of salvation; her hair was brushed and gleaming; she was wearing her favourite hair clips and she looked clean and pretty, not bruised and rumpled and messed up from a wild ride and a rough landing.

"You see!" said Josie triumphantly. "I knew we were right to come!"

"Awesome!" said Dusty.

"But it's not right," said Henrietta, scared of what was happening.

"I've never looked so good," said Dusty, considering himself from all angles. "This is exactly what I want to look like!"

"But it *can* be what you look like," said Josie. "Don't you see?"

"No," said Henrietta shortly. "That just sounds like mumbo-jumbo."

"Well, you would say that!" snapped Josie.

"Uh, I don't think it can really be true," said Dusty slowly. But it was clear the river was having an overwhelming effect on both Josie and Dusty. They seemed unable to resist the pull of the Self.

"No," said Hugo as firmly as he could. "No, this isn't right at all!"

"I think that the river shows you as you want to see yourself," said Henrietta, turning her face reluctantly away from her reflection and fingering the Bible at her side.

"That's it, Henry!" said Hugo. "It's like the Water of Sound Doctrine, but the opposite!"

"That makes no sense at all," said Josie. "I suppose you know that."

"The Water of Sound Doctrine shows you as the Bible sees you; it shows the true you as you are inside," said Hugo. "But the water of the River Self only shows you as you want to see yourself – all the outside bits – all perfect and lovely with no faults or problems at all! But it can never be true. It's lying to you!"

"This is too weird," said Dusty.

"I think that's why Bourne warned us against the river," said Henrietta.

"Let's go back," urged Hugo. "We need to go back, come on Josie!"

"In a moment," said Josie dreamily. "Just let me think what to do."

"The words 'think' and 'Josie' in the same sentence always give me a bad feeling," Hugo muttered to Henrietta.

Henrietta watched her cousin looking fixedly at the River Self. She saw Dusty's struggle to allow the Truth he had learned from the Bible to overcome his trust in himself and his own ideas.

"Remember what Bourne said about only God being worthy of our confidence and trust?" said Henrietta.

Slowly Dusty turned his eyes away from his fixed reflection in the river. "Let's get out of here," he said, "before we all fall in!"

Josie reluctantly followed the others away from the river, dragging her heels. Hugo and Henrietta were only glad that she was following them at all. What they would do if Josie was lost in the River Self didn't bear thinking about. There was no way they could rescue her from that greedy water.

Darkness was around them but it was not hard to find the road that led through the outskirts of the town of Alternative Teaching. Hugo took a Locator out of his pocket. He had cleverly extracted it from the Capsule. The Locator didn't seem to be affected by the

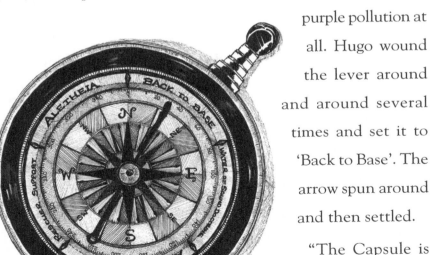

purple pollution at all. Hugo wound the lever around and around several times and set it to 'Back to Base'. The arrow spun around and then settled.

"The Capsule is this way," said Hugo.

"We can go down this road through the town and branch off into the trees."

The town was deathly quiet as they walked through it. Neat houses with nice gardens stood on either side of the road, but no one was in sight. The houses and gardens were slightly odd in places, but the children took no notice of the chimney which stuck out from a wall, or the completely round door, or the house whose walls appeared to be made of grass. They didn't even stop to look at the knives and forks planted neatly in the garden by someone who was experimenting with an alternative method of adding to their cutlery collection. The townspeople of Alternative Teaching seemed to be shut up in their homes, with all the curtains drawn in the windows.

"Perhaps they're trying to keep the smell out," said Dusty.

"I know I would if I could!" said Henrietta.

"I wonder if they know about the storm," said Hugo. "Perhaps they're afraid of it."

They didn't linger in the town; there was really nothing to stop for. All the shops were shut and only once did they see any sign of life, which was when someone twitched aside a curtain and then hastily pulled it shut again. Hugo's Locator didn't let them down. The arrow on the round dial moved and showed them the path they should take through the trees outside the town. The children drew closer together as they walked through the trees and the darkness. The purple was increasing and there were stirrings around them that made them shiver. They were very glad when the large Capsule came into view. They hurried to the door.

"I never thought I'd be so glad to get back!" exclaimed Dusty.

"Let's get in and lock the door," said Henrietta.

"We'll have some food and then get to bed," said Hugo.

"There are still some cookies," said Henrietta as she clambered through the door.

Dusty entered next and flung himself thankfully into one of the comfy armchairs.

Hugo came through the door, and then sudden, disquieting silence descended on them. No one wanted to break it; no one wanted to ask the question that needed to be asked.

Where was Josie?

CHAPTER 14
A CALL FOR HELP

Hugo, pale and looking pretty sick, carefully followed the instructions that Bourne had left him for contacting the Central Control Room in Aletheia via the Capsule's Mission Detector. He figured he had no choice but to ask for help. There was no doubt about it: Josie had gone.

Hugo sat in the pilot's chair and watched as the Capsule's big screen spluttered reluctantly into life. There was a 'low battery' indicator flashing at the top of the screen. Hugo ignored that. He pulled the lever until 'Central Control Room, Aletheia' showed on the screen. He pressed the 'Contact' button, and all three children held a collective breath as the screen flashed a sick looking green, and then, "Capsule Three-Sixteen, come in; Capsule Three-Sixteen..."

"Uh...is that Brian?" asked Hugo.

"Control Room Manager, Mr Brian Buffer, speaking; Capsule Three-Sixteen, you are showing low battery for this exchange."

"We know that," said Hugo. "We need some help."

There was a momentary pause. Then, "Please clarify: is this

a point of policy, procedure or practice?"

"Uh, just some advice please," said Hugo.

"Proceed, Three-Sixteen," said Brian. He sounded faintly puzzled.

"It's Hugo Wallop speaking," said Hugo. "Lieutenant Bourne Faithful and Private Harold Wallop have gone to the Standfirms' Emergency Rendezvous point. We're in the Capsule…"

"He knows that bit!" whispered Henrietta.

Hugo glared at her.

"Sorry," she muttered.

"We have lost Josie Faithful," said Hugo.

"Lost?" faltered Brian.

Henrietta sighed. "I didn't think he was going to be the quickest in emergencies," she murmured dolefully to Dusty.

"I think I should go and get her," said Hugo.

"Do you?" said Brian.

"We need to know if that's alright," said Hugo. "Or what else we should do."

"Uh…Capsule Three-Sixteen, stand by; we're checking procedures for, uh, lost Rescuer Personnel…"

"I don't think Josie is Rescuer Personnel exactly," whispered Henrietta.

Hugo shrugged somewhat helplessly.

"Uh, Hugo?" said Brian.

"Yes, Brian," said Hugo.

Henrietta smothered a sudden giggle that threatened to burst from her. Hugo sounded so funny and grown-up, and he really should have called Brian 'Mr Buffer', or 'Sir', shouldn't he?

"Clarify the profile of lost Josie Faithful?" queried Brian.

"Umm, she goes to school," said Hugo.

There was a pause. "Uh, we don't have, uh, a protocol that answers to your, uh, exact situation," said Brian.

"I didn't think so," muttered Henrietta.

"Can you let us know what you think anyway?" said Hugo.

"He only knows it if it's in a procedure!" whispered Henrietta.

"Uh, we have not got enough information to provide a quick procedure for you to follow in this, uh, most unforeseen event," said Brian. "Please clarify what your Risk Assessment grading was for this mission?"

"Risk Assessment?" exclaimed Hugo.

Henrietta was biting her hands to keep from exploding in undignified, hysterical laughter.

"We usually expect a Risk Assessment to be filed before, uh, a rescue mission that involves minors," said Brian.

"That makes us sound as if we live underground," said Dusty.

Henrietta almost exploded and made a weird noise that sounded a bit like a sneeze. Hugo glared at her and she quickly sobered up. "Don't make me laugh!" she whispered to Dusty.

"Look, can you just let Bourne and Harold know what's happened?" asked Hugo.

"Uh, Capsule Three-Sixteen, what exactly *has* happened? Clarify details please."

The low battery indicator was now flashing red in a most urgent manner. Then suddenly the screen went blank and there was nothing.

"Great!" said Hugo. "Just great! Fat lot of good that was! We should have used the battery to search for the location of Bourne and Harold!"

"Well, at least you've told that man Brian about Josie and to let Bourne and Harold know what's happened," said Dusty.

"Let's hope Brian doesn't need a procedure to understand that much!" said Henrietta.

"I think we'll just have to find Josie on our own!" said Hugo.

None of them really wanted to leave the safety of the Capsule and venture out into the night to rescue Josie. Hugo thought he must go. He was in charge; and somehow he must find her. He didn't persuade the others to come but, all the same, he was glad when they both refused to be left behind.

"It'll be dangerous for you, Dusty," warned Hugo. "You don't have the protection we have. Stay inside the Capsule and wait for us."

Dusty couldn't see the armour of God[16] that the twins wore, because he wasn't a Christian. He didn't know about the helmet of salvation which kept the Christian's mind focussed on the greatness of the salvation that God had provided for them; he didn't know that the body armour guarded the Christian's heart and feelings; that the belt of Truth surrounded them and kept them from the false gods that were even now out there in the storm; that the sturdy gospel boots took them to places in order to bring the good news about the Lord Jesus; and that the shield of faith helped them to trust completely and absolutely in God alone and in no one else, least of all themselves.

But Dusty could see the Bibles the twins carried at their sides. He knew that Hugo and Henrietta believed that this book, the Bible, was the living and powerful Word of God[24]. How else would they dare to go into such a storm with only that as their weapon? Dusty realised that he certainly wasn't enough in himself to go out into the purple storm. There must be something else that could help him.

"Couldn't I carry a Bible?" asked Dusty.

Hugo looked surprised, but he quickly retrieved a Bible from the store of goods that Bourne and Harold had been unable to carry and handed it to Dusty. Dusty looked at it in silence. It didn't really seem to be anything at all: just a book. It didn't glow with light like the ones that both Hugo and Henrietta carried. But Dusty put it in his pocket anyway.

And that was how they set out: the twins in their armour with their Bibles in their pouches at their sides, and Dusty with a Bible he wasn't sure he believed in secure in his pocket. They followed the dim trail through the wood to the River Self. It seemed obvious to all three of them that that was where Josie had returned; she had seemed so intent on the river, and they thought that she might even have ventured across the bridge.

"We'll walk down the river until we come to the bridge that Harold and Bourne took," said Hugo. "But remember, don't look in the water!"

It didn't take them long. They hurried through the darkness. There were strange stirrings in the trees around them. None of them commented, although all of them noticed, the dominant purple hue around them. Already it was much increased. When they stood on the road, where the bridge spanned the River Self, there was a terrible silence amongst them. Henrietta clutched Hugo, and Dusty put his hand in his pocket and touched the Bible that lay there.

The River Self had risen; the water was raging beyond control; purple mist was all around; the bridge was broken and gone.

None of them said the words out loud. None of them said what they were all thinking: that Josie might have been taken by the rushing torrent of the greedy River Self, sucked under by the grasping tendrils and rolled away on the swelling waves. None of them said the word *drowned*.

"It's...it's pulling at me!" said Dusty.

"Back to the Capsule!" said Hugo decisively.

"It *is* tugging," said Henrietta. "I feel it too! We're being pulled towards the river!"

They stepped away from the river banks. Dusty wanted no part of the raging water any more than the twins did. He was beginning to question all the things he had thought about himself and how he could figure out all the answers about where to live, how to live, what to believe. If self was like that greedy, uncontrolled, deadly river, all rushing mindlessly in the same direction, then he didn't want it at all. It seemed there was no solution in self; it would merely consume you until you were utterly ruined. And it didn't make him any different, or any better, than anyone else. All who relied on themselves were going the same way. The solution of peace and happiness and everything else certainly did not lie there.

"Back to the Capsule," Hugo urged.

"It's all very well saying *back to the Capsule* like that, but getting there is a different matter!" said Henrietta.

She was right. As easy as it had been to take the path to the River Self, it was like walking into a strong headwind to go away from it. But there was no wind.

"It's like a magnet pulls you there, and a force-field blocks you on the way back!" panted Dusty.

The twins found that they were walking more easily in their protective armour of God than Dusty could manage, even though it was still like walking through thick, sticky mud. But Dusty could barely take a step away from the river. They took an arm each and the three of them fought the strange, compelling power that was pulling them back to the Self. In silence they reached the trees and held onto each other as they walked down the trail to the Capsule. They stumbled through the door and Hugo shut it tight. They pushed a supply crate against the door and only then did they sink into the armchairs and look at each other across the dimness of the unlit cabin. No one could have said what had frightened them, but they were certain that there were unknown creatures out there, gathering in the purple darkness: things they could not see but knew they must flee from.

"What now?" asked Henrietta at last.

"We sleep," said Hugo.

"Uh…" Dusty hesitated. "Do you think you should pray?" he asked. "I mean, all that talk about prayer power and stuff, do you think it might help against…whatever is out there?"

"Uh, yes," said Hugo hastily. "Of course. That's exactly what we need to do now, before, uh, we go to sleep."

Dusty watched the twins through half shut eyes. After a few stuttering sentences, they spoke as if they knew the God they asked to help them. They seemed to think that this God of the Bible could defeat the strange power of the purple storm; they seemed to think that He could see and rescue Josie from whatever had befallen her in the land of Err. Dusty wondered what it would be like to stop trusting in himself and totally rely on the God of the Bible, the God who was all-powerful and all-knowing, the God who had even made him[13]. This was the God who loved him and showed grace to him despite the fact that he had never paid Him any attention and had even considered discounting Him entirely.

"The Bible," Dusty said suddenly when the twins finished praying. "It's lit up! It's shining!"

He was looking with awe at the Bible in his hand.

"I think that means that you're beginning to be willing to be guided by it, Dusty," said Hugo wonderingly. "You're beginning to realise that it can be a light for you and show you the way."

It was the only explanation. Up until now the Bible that Dusty held had not shown light. It wasn't that it was any different or any less true than the Bibles that Hugo and Henrietta carried, but when Dusty began to think about the message of the Bible and about what the Lord Jesus had done, now, suddenly, there was light in his hand.

They each took blankets from the supplies and settled into one of the comfortable reclining armchairs. There was silence around them. Nothing seemed to be beyond the Capsule and, apart from the ever present smell, they might have thought the storm was past. They all fell deeply asleep.

Dusty slept with his hand on the Bible.

CHAPTER 15
THE SURPRISE FLIGHT

The children awoke to an almighty CRASH! The purple storm was upon them! All three of them scrambled hastily from their blankets, no longer even slightly sleepy, suddenly horribly awake. They stared out of the Capsule's round windows. It was night, and yet there was a strange glow with an unmistakably purple tint outside of the windows.

CRASH!

Another tree went tumbling to the ground and the Capsule trembled.

"Hugo!" said Henrietta. "What shall we do?"

It was a good question but not exactly a helpful one for Hugo. Already Josie had vanished on his watch, and they had barely dragged Dusty away from the compelling tug of the River Self. Now they were in danger of being crushed by falling trees, captive in a damaged Capsule that couldn't even fly.

"We stay put," said Hugo grimly. "There's nothing else to do."

"What if a tree falls on us??"

"Do you have any better ideas?" asked Hugo, horrified at the sight of falling trees and billowing purple clouds, and...strange shapes...or *something*...

"We have to stay here," said Dusty. There was a tremble in his voice. "Did you just see that...was it a ghost?" he asked aghast.

"I don't think there are any such things as ghosts," said Hugo more certainly than he felt.

"Don't look," said Henrietta. "Remember what Bourne said about the storm being full of false creatures that people trust in. We've got to focus on what the Bible teaches about God!"

The wind shrieked angrily around the Capsule. It seemed to have a voice: a cruel, chilling voice. Suddenly the Capsule was lifted on the arms of the fierce wind. It rose, and then fell again, crunching to the ground. The three children went spinning across the floor.

"Hugo!" said Henrietta.

"There's nothing I can do, Henry!" said Hugo.

"Shouldn't you...uh, what about praying again?" asked Dusty. He remembered how comforted he felt the last time the twins prayed out loud to the God of the Bible. If God was everything that the Bible said about Him, if He alone was worthy of people's faith, then God could certainly save them from the storm.

"Yes, we'll pray!" said Hugo. "But grab hold of something and hang on, we're on the move again…hang on! Up we go!…Henry, PRAY…!!"

They didn't know how long they spun and whirled about the sky. They hardly knew whether they were upside down, inside out, left or right or anything else. They all clutched the small rings around the peepholes in the floor of the Capsule and hung on for dear life.

But suddenly there was a surprisingly gentle *crunch*…and the Capsule lay silent and still. From everything that was loud and terrifying, to sudden nothingness. Incredibly they had landed safely on the ground. And more astonishing still, instantly there was no noise of the awful wind or really of anything at all. It was completely silent.

Slowly, tremblingly, the three children got up from the floor of the Capsule and gingerly stood on their feet.

"Where do you think we are?" asked Henrietta faintly.

Hugo was staring out of the window with a stunned expression on his face. Outside was night but there were comforting lights and lanterns lighting a large enclosure. There was no purple in sight. All around was orderly and calm. They had landed in the middle of an organised campsite.

"I think," Hugo said slowly and with disbelief very evident in his tone, "I think we've landed in the middle of the Emergency Rendezvous!"

"Awesome!" said Dusty. He picked up the Bible. "Imagine God being able to do that!" he said.

Hugo led the way from the Capsule and the three children stood staring at the calm, clear, lit enclosure. Around them were transport vehicles of various kinds, with the unmistakable stamp of the Rescuers about them. There were a few large tents, one with strange wires and contraptions sticking up into the air. They knew this would be the mobile Communications Centre. There were also lots of smaller tents. There were boxes and crates in orderly piles, and tables and stalls near some of them with supplies neatly displayed, as if they were just waiting for people to arrive and use them. One of the tables contained Water of Sound Doctrine in bottles; one contained Bibles and spare armour; another had blankets and clothing. The Capsule had landed just about in the centre of the enclosure, and yet without touching any of the surrounding supplies. In fact, it was just as if it was intended to be parked exactly where it was!

Close by the Capsule was a Rescuer Atob. This was a sturdy three-wheeled vehicle with a large steering wheel, an onboard Mission Detector, and comfortable seats facing front and back. There was no roof, but there was a frame for one sticking up in the air and somewhere there would be a roof canvas neatly rolled away, ready to shelter the Atob from bad weather. The twins and Dusty were familiar with Atobs. They were common in the land of Err and were simply a vehicle intended to take someone from A to B. They weren't the fastest, most robust way to travel – although the Rescuer Atobs were by far the most reliable in Err — but they were dependable enough, and this one was full of fuel and ready to drive. It was as if it had been prepared for their use.

Hugo powered up the Mission Detector in the Atob and first checked for the whereabouts of Harold and Bourne. The screen flickered to life and the words 'Private Harold Wallop: Status — Active; Location — Other-gods Conference Centre' flashed onto the screen. And for Bourne it was similar: 'Lieutenant Bourne Faithful: Status — Active, Group Leader; Location — Other-gods Conference Centre'.

"They're busy in the storm," said Henrietta. "They can't help us now."

Hugo wrote the name 'Josie Faithful' on the screen with his finger. The Detector took its time. It flashed the word 'working' on and off the screen as if it wasn't quite sure about Josie. The three children held their breath as at last a map appeared upon which was a small, white dot.

"Hurray!" said Henrietta.

"She didn't drown!" said Dusty, somewhat surprised.

"I'm not sure she's exactly praying for help," said Hugo, examining the information on the screen. Both Hugo and Henrietta knew that to rescue someone in Err they had to *want* to be rescued. They had to pray for help, and then the Rescuers were sent to help them.

"She must be praying," said Henrietta. "That's why it shows where she is!"

"No," said Hugo. "I think…perhaps Brian has entered her name into the Mission Detector system to be rescued as part of the purple storm mission. I think that's why she shows!"

"Well, no matter why it shows where Josie is," said Henrietta, "let's go and get her!"

Hugo was hesitating and weighing the decision to go after Josie. Outside of the strange stillness and clarity of the Emergency Rendezvous, they could clearly see a bank of threatening purple clouds all around. It was as if the storm was surrounding the Rescuers' enclosure but was unable to get in. Hugo knew this was because the Emergency Rendezvous was protected with prayer. But once they left the safety of the enclosure there would be no such protection.

"Perhaps you should stay here," Hugo said to Dusty. He knew that no harm could befall Dusty here. There was invisible prayer protection all around.

"No," said Dusty. "I've come this far, I'm going to stick with you."

"But you don't have the protection of the armour of God," said Hugo.

"I know that," said Dusty. "But God has answered your prayers until now, and if He can do this..." he gestured around the calm, protected enclosure, "well then, I guess He can protect us in the storm too!"

It was hard to argue with that, and, despite Hugo's vague misgivings, all three of them climbed aboard the Atob. Hugo pressed the 'Start' button confidently. He didn't want the others to know how uncertain he was about driving the Rescuer Atob.

'For advice about location press here', flashed across the Mission Detector screen.

Hugo pressed the word 'here' on the screen. All three children leaned in to read what was displayed on the screen:

'Please be advised you are entering a Danger Zone'.

"I've never heard of a Danger Zone!" exclaimed Henrietta. "I do think Harold should tell us more about Rescuer stuff!"

And then more information filled the Detector screen.

'In the location of Other-gods Conference Centre people have faith in anything and often create gods of their own ideas and in their own image. These creatures may be judgemental, selfish, demanding, capricious, violent and vicious. Or they may seem beautiful and rich and enticing.'

"It makes them sound so real," said Henrietta with a shudder. And then they all read the next sentence on the screen.

'Be warned that the creatures that people invent may seem to appear in physical form.'

"That's what Bourne warned us against!" said Hugo.

'Mysterious, unsubstantiated reports circulate regarding the exact nature of this. The Academy of Soldiers-of-the-Cross has not ruled out the false gods of people's imaginings actually appearing in various physical forms, but there has been limited opportunity to study this. Occurrences of physical creatures are likely to be infrequent in a red storm, and most frequent in a rare purple storm.'

"Great," groaned Henrietta.

"Well, we already knew that the purple storm is the worst," said Hugo.

'The following advice is offered to Rescuers entering this Danger Zone:

1. Take all normal routine precautions, e.g. Armour of God, Water of Sound Doctrine etc.

2. Focus your mind constantly on the one, true God;

3. Memorise appropriate verses from the Bible, e.g. about the character of God;

4. Ensure maximum prayer power support at all times in the Danger Zone.'

"Well, I've always got Mrs De Voté's prayers," said Henrietta, more confidently than she felt. She didn't doubt that Mrs De Voté meant well, but could one little old lady praying really make that much of a difference against the purple storm?

"I hope this Mrs De Voté is some kind of magician," said Dusty.

"What did you say, Henry?" asked Hugo vaguely. He was thinking about their mission. And the description of the Mission Detector regarding what might lie ahead did not fill him with confidence.

But somewhere out there, in the purple darkness, subjected to the unknown terrors of the storm, Josie might be desperate for help. In subdued silence the Atob slipped out of the fresh air of the Emergency Rendezvous and into the bank of vile smelling black and purple clouds.

CHAPTER 16
IN THE GRIP OF THE STORM

It was like passing from day into night; from a nice dream into a nightmare; from the real, sane world, into another one entirely, where your worst fears come true. The wind was all around them, not in one direction or another, not like a normal wind at all. It was sweeping the foul, purple clouds into their faces, chasing the clouds round and round, or up and down, or into dangerous funnels which could sweep them into the air at any moment the way it had done with the Capsule. At other times it would drop into unexpected, uncanny silence and then suddenly terrify them with wild shrieks that contained voices they didn't want to hear.

The Atob had started well in the protected Rescuer enclosure but the further it travelled into the purple smoke and mist and cloud, the more sluggish it became. The purple pollution was sapping its energy. It limped slowly and falteringly, seeming ready to give up altogether and leave them all at the mercy of the storm.

Worse than the smell, and the unpredictable, dangerous wind, just beyond the Atob's wavering lights were the shapes and the voices which belonged to the creatures that were part of the storm.

"They're not real, Henry," Hugo said to his trembling sister when the wind died down just enough to hear each other speak. "Remember, they're not real. They are the things that people trust in when they refuse to acknowledge the true God."

"Think of Bible verses," pleaded Henrietta. "Say them out loud, Hugo!"

But the wind rose with a terrible cry and Hugo's words were carried away.

"Think of them in your head, Henry!" he yelled.

Henrietta sat shaking, too frightened to think of what was happening to Dusty who was sitting on the seat behind. She tried to recall the wonderful things she knew about the God of Heaven who was everything that was light[25] and love; unchanging, all-knowing, perfect in holiness and justice; the One who alone was worthy of their faith and trust[13]. Around them the creatures of people's false imagining raged and roared. Unpredictable, changeable, false, unjust, demanding, selfish: just a reflection of what people were themselves.

Henrietta closed her eyes for a moment and thought of how

the purple storm had appeared from the foot of the cross where she had first seen it. The storm had seemed so small, and it *was* a small thing compared to the storm that the Lord Jesus had passed through when He bore the punishment for her sins. And because the Lord Jesus had done that for her, and brought her back to God[5], God was her refuge in the storm. "God is our refuge and strength,[23]" murmured Henrietta. She had once learned Psalm 46 at school and, in the fright of the storm, she could only recall verse 1; but it was enough to comfort her. "God is our refuge and strength..."

Dusty clutched the sides of his chair in the back of the Atob in abject terror. The creatures in the storm were very real to him. In some twisted, inexplicable way solid beings seemed to form out of the purple mist and darkness. They descended on him, taunting him that they were real and true and that he could trust in them. The creatures, these gods that people invented out of their own desire to trust in other things apart from the one, true God[22], took many shapes and seemed to be many different things – both wonderful and terrible. There were plenty of hideous monsters that would devour Dusty in their wide, gaping mouths. Some had massive, grasping hands; some had horrible, pitiless mouths; some had vile, shrivelling breath; some had cruel nails and claws. They were creatures that were characterised by Greed, and Hate, and Blasphemy, and Power. And the monstrous creature with the enormous head, bulging, pulsing brain, and unblinking, penetrating eyes was Self: a creature that thought it was all-knowing and all-seeing, just like God.

There were beautiful and enticing shapes in the storm too. When Dusty shrank from the hideous monsters, these more appealing creatures came to him. Some of these were dripping with glittering gold and jewels and carrying chains to ensnare and trap; some had wide, welcoming smiles and really seemed to like him. One even blew him kisses that had the unforgettable odour of the purple pollution and made him feel sick. There were even beings that seemed to depict famous, rich, religious, beautiful, desirable people, most of whom were long dead and gone from the world.

All of the creatures, whether beautiful or monstrous, enticed Dusty to consider them as worthy of his faith and trust.

Dusty tightly clutched the Bible in his hand. It was the only source of light and comfort in that horror of tormenting thoughts and doubts about what and in whom he could trust.

Suddenly a monster swept down upon him, leering at him from a swirling purple cloud. It was the monster with the hideous pulsing brain. *"Self!"* shrieked the monster's eerie voice, just like the shriek of the wind. *"I am everything!"*

Dusty cowered in horror. The shape immediately changed and became a nice, smiling man with a gold chain around his neck and gold and jewels on his fingers. "You are clever enough, Dusty," he said. "You can make your own fortune like me! Riches will make you happy and bring you peace, you'll see!" The man reached out a finger with a diamond ring upon it and flicked the Bible that was in Dusty's hand.

The Bible slipped from Dusty's fingers and fell with a thud to the floor of the Atob. Dusty stared at the man.

"The Bible won't do anything to help you, Dusty," the man said kindly. "That book was written hundreds of years ago. There's nothing in it that will help you today!"

Very faintly, from the front of the Atob, Dusty heard Henrietta's voice murmuring, "God is our refuge..." He remembered what the twins and Bourne and Harold thought about the Bible. That it was a living[24] book because God had inspired it[21]. It didn't matter how long ago the Bible was written. It was *living* and that meant it wasn't out of date at all!

For a moment Dusty turned his gaze from the smiling man and looked at the steady, bright, white, light of the Bible that now lay on the floor of the Atob. The Bible alone seemed untouched by the purple horror and pollution around.

"Oh true God of grace and mercy, help me!" cried Dusty.

The nice, smiling man-shape shattered into a thousand pieces! The bits that had been the man – the gold chain, the jewels, even the fixed smile – were carried away on the wind of the storm. The Bible glowed triumphantly on the floor of the Atob and, trembling, Dusty picked it up once more. Around him the horror of the storm continued, but he had lost some of the terror of it.

"Oh God, I don't really know the right words," said Dusty, "but they tell me that You will forgive me because of grace, because You sent Your Son the Lord Jesus who came to die so my sins could be forgiven. I'd like to accept what the Lord Jesus did for me and forget about myself. I want all my faith to be in You only from now on."

The Atob was moving ever more slowly down the track into the storm. Then it stopped altogether. The wind dropped to one of its sudden, uncanny silences. Hugo looked at the Mission Detector screen in consternation.

"It says, '*Arrived at destination*'!" he said.

"Some destination!" Henrietta managed to say from chattering teeth. "It must have made a mistake!"

They were close enough to the ceremony taking place in a huge open-air arena at the Other-gods Conference Centre to see the large screen flickering in front of crowds of wailing people. The image of a man, the dead footballer called Lincoln Lionheart, was projected on the screen. The distant echo of loud, thumping music rose and fell on the wind.

"It's awful," said Henrietta.

"They have no hope," said Hugo, appalled at the masses focussed on a dead man. "He can't help them!"

"Uh, I think there's something over there," said Dusty falteringly. He had seen a faint trail through some shrubs at the side of the road. The trail led to a small alcove that flickered with uncertain, ghostly light. The small sign at the side of the road said, '*This way to grotto of movie star, Melody.*'

"We've reached Josie!" said Hugo.

"That's why the Atob stopped here!" said Henrietta.

They all clambered quickly from the Atob and, sticking very close together, they pressed through the shrubs to the alcove which was dedicated to Melody, the movie star. Alone, huddled trembling on the floor and sobbing uncontrollably, was Josie. Above her, gleaming weirdly in the flickering candlelight was a small golden statue of beautiful Melody.

"Josie!" exclaimed Henrietta. She fell to her knees beside her cousin on the floor. "Come on, Josie, we've come to take you home."

Josie didn't move. She didn't seem to hear. They poked and prodded and whispered and even shouted, but nothing moved her from her tightly curled position on the floor. It was as if she couldn't see anything but the terror of the purple storm that was all about her; it was as if she couldn't hear anything but the false voices calling to her on the cruel wind.

Dusty tentatively uncurled his fingers from the Bible that was glowing with strong, pure light in his hands. He opened its pages and the light spilled around them, warming them with its bright rays.

"Good!" said Hugo, not stopping to wonder at the unmistakable light that now shone from Dusty's Bible. A light that strong could only mean one thing: that Dusty had trusted in the God of the Bible and had his sins taken away through the sacrifice of the Lord Jesus. He was willing to be guided by the Bible now.

"Pray!" urged Henrietta. The creatures of the storm did not like the light of the Bible but they were still crowding and jostling around the open doorway to the grotto, as if at any moment they might enter and overcome them all. Henrietta looked around frantically for a weapon. What could defeat these creatures of evil imaginations? She picked up a stone. Alone it could do nothing, but what if she threw it believing that God would help them? She remembered the square of uninspiring, unfinished knitting that Mrs De Voté had given her what felt like a lifetime ago. It was the old lady's pledge that she was praying for them too. As the storm renewed its shriek and a monstrous creature reached a greedy hand towards them where they were huddled in the grotto, Henrietta placed her stone in the centre of the knitted square. Using the loose strands of wool at the corners, she secured the stone, swung it around like a sling, and catapulted it towards the heart of the purple storm.

Usually Henrietta didn't throw particularly well. Hugo always said she threw "just like a girl!" But instead of dropping to the ground or hitting the walls of the grotto, the stone flew out of the knitted square like a rocket and shattered the purple darkness with the most tremendous BANG!

And it didn't stop there.

White, gold, and silver sparks lit up the air around the grotto, showering light and beauty all around them. It was just like the most wonderful, unexpected fireworks display. When the sparks died away, around and about the four children was clear, pure air. They were contained in a bubble, just like they had been in

the Emergency Rendezvous enclosure. Josie was still dazed but the unpolluted air was reviving her and she was responding to them, allowing them to help her from the alcove. All around them was the clear, fresh air of the 'bubble'; just beyond it they could see the purple billows and the wild storm and the swirling, angry shapes. But there was no fear in it for them. One of the monsters even banged his large, ugly fists on the outside of the bubble. But it made not the smallest dent in the solid, clear calm that now surrounded the children.

Wonderingly, almost silently, the four children took their seats in the Atob. With the protection of Mrs De Voté's prayers around them, they started up the Atob and drove back down the road to the Rescuers' enclosure. The Atob went easily and smoothly, happy and raring to go. It was no longer hampered by the purple pollution, and nor were the children.

"What exactly *was* that?" asked Dusty in a hushed, awed tone.

"Prayer," said Henrietta in an equally awestruck tone. "Mrs De Voté is praying!"

"She must be a very strong lady!" said Dusty.

"No," said Henrietta wonderingly. "No, she's not really that at all."

"Oh," said Dusty.

"What I mean is that I think it's her faith – her absolute confidence in God – that did this," said Henrietta. "She trusted so much in God's power, that He did *this*!" She gestured to the protective bubble around them.

"I think God must love to be trusted," said Dusty.

"Yes," said Henrietta. Then she looked at Dusty. "Do you believe in the Lord Jesus now, Dusty?"

"Yes," said Dusty. "I believe."

CHAPTER 17
A STRANGE GATHERING

The four children returned to the Rescue Capsule without incident. The Emergency Rendezvous enclosure was as quiet and deserted as when they had left it. There was no one else in sight. The Rescuers were still out in the storm reaching the people who were crying for help to the one true God. The Rescuers' support teams – the drivers, engineers, communication people, assistants, cooks and whoever else had come to support this great mission – were either with them or sleeping peacefully in some of the many tents and shelters.

The children climbed wearily through the door of the damaged Capsule and collapsed into the comfortable reclining armchairs. No one spoke much, Josie least of all. She was pale and silent, and fell asleep immediately. None of the children felt in any danger. All was secure around them. One by one, they fell into a deep, peaceful, dreamless sleep with Mrs De Voté's prayer protection, as well as the prayer protection arranged around the large enclosure, like a soft blanket around them. It was as if all the knitted squares that Mrs De Voté had ever made now lay quietly upon them, and no one could unpick those even strands and disturb that calm.

When the children awoke it was to a different scene, almost a different world. Sunshine was streaming through the small, round windows on one half of the Capsule. The night and the storm were over. Small wisps of purple smoke trailed harmlessly beyond the Rescuers' enclosure. Some purple vapour still lay like a dirty cloud over the buildings of the Other-gods Conference Centre in the distance. The road beyond the enclosure was well trodden and muddy and there was a slight tinge of purple to the mud. The distant River Self was an unhealthy purple hue, as if it felt rather sick. But that was all there was to see of the purple storm. The threat of it was past; the destruction of it was over. The four children stood bewildered in the open doorway of the Capsule, blinking in the bright sunshine, and breathing in the fresh, odourless air. Around them was the most astonishing scene.

If they hadn't known that they were at the scene of a large rescue mission, they might, said Henrietta, imagine that a strange circus had arrived and surrounded them sometime in the night.

Certainly the activity around them had all the marks of the most extraordinary event.

The tables and stalls and supplies and tents were no longer silent. Around the Capsule, in every direction, there were dozens and dozens of people: milling around, talking, laughing, eating and drinking. There were tables serving hot drinks and cold drinks; a stand where someone was cooking sausages and making big pancakes; a stall where someone was handing out blankets and big warm jackets. There were ordinary people there, battered and tattered and dirty, wrapped in the blankets and jackets of the Rescuers. These were people that had prayed for rescue from their dreadful decision to trust in a dead football star instead of the true God of the Bible. Now they looked relieved and joyful. There were other people there who looked confused and tired. They were relieved to have escaped the storm, but they didn't know if they were willing to trust in the God of the Bible. There were tired and hungry support staff, and big, burly Rescuers looking weary but relieved.

"I see Harold," cried Henrietta, pointing through the crowd.

"I smell sausages and bacon!" said Hugo.

"I'm hungry," said Dusty. "And I'd really like to try some of that water you like to drink!"

Hugo laughed and clapped Dusty on the back. They all felt happy with joy and relief. Well, perhaps Josie didn't feel quite so happy. It was hard to tell what Josie was thinking.

"You go on," she said quietly to the others. "I'll join you in a bit." And then Josie vanished inside the Capsule again.

Henrietta knew that Josie wanted to be alone. The other three children made their way to where Harold stood waving at them and eating a bacon roll.

"So, you're awake at last!" said Harold with a grin.

"I suppose you knew we were all safely in the Capsule fast asleep!" said Henrietta.

"Of course!" said Harold.

"Well, if they didn't know, I hope they'd be out there looking for us, not eating bacon rolls!" said Dusty.

"You can't do anything without a Mission Detector

spotting you!" said Henrietta. But no one was complaining about that.

"Brian is a busy man," said Hugo drily.

"I think Brian is also a confused man," said Harold. "We received a message about your request for advice from the Control Room. I don't think Brian knew quite what to make of it."

"It wasn't in a procedure," said Henrietta.

"It's because we were minors," said Dusty.

Henrietta giggled. Anything and everything might make her laugh on this victorious, sunny morning.

"I'm afraid the call to the Control Room didn't really help," said Hugo.

"Well, never mind about that," said Harold. "You did well, Hugo!"

Hugo went a bit red and looked really chuffed. "I hope you don't get into trouble for not completing a Risk Assessment," he said.

Harold merely shrugged. "Who needs a Risk Assessment when people pray?" he said.

"Mrs De Voté is my answer to a Risk Assessment," said Henrietta.

"I must hear the details about that," said Harold. "But first..." and he pushed the three children towards the mounds of bacon and sausages and fresh bread rolls that were nearby.

"Is this the same as the bacon that the security man Jeff was eating when we first arrived at the Academy of Soldiers-of-the-Cross?" asked Dusty.

"I believe it might be," said Harold, amused at the question. "All of our food comes from the Pray-Always Farmlands in Aletheia."

"Whatever made you think of that?" asked Hugo.

"Oh, nothing really," said Dusty. "I guess I was just thinking that if I go through that Contamination Detector again hopefully the alarm won't go off! I don't think I'm contaminated anymore!"

"I take it that you have become a Christian, Dusty," said Harold with a smile.

"You haven't told us when it happened," said Henrietta.

"Well," said Dusty, "I hope I am a Christian, but I didn't know the right words to say. I told God that I knew that His Son came to die so that my sins could be forgiven and that I'd like to accept what He did and forget about myself. Do you think that's enough?"

"Absolutely enough!" said Harold. "It's not really about the right words and *you* doing enough, it's just about putting your faith – your whole trust and confidence – in what the Lord Jesus has done to save you. And what He has done is more than enough![26]"

"Awesome!" said Dusty. "God saved me just like that and I had been so dead set against Him! I know what grace means now: God accepted me when I didn't deserve it at all!"

"And besides," added Harold, "if you want proof, there is very real proof that you have been saved and are now a Christian!"

"Is there?"

Harold nodded. "You're looking at it," he said.

Dusty looked at the cup of crystal clear water that he held in his hand. He took another sip of it. He kept sipping it again and again, and when he wasn't drinking it he was looking at it as if it was too good to be true. "Awesome!" he kept saying. "So clean; and just the right taste!"

"The fact that you desire the Water of Sound Doctrine is

proof that you are saved," said Harold. "That is the water that represents the whole Truth of the Bible. How you see and enjoy that water shows you how you see and appreciate the Word of God. Every true work of God will result in a desire for the Word of God!"

They ate so many delicious sausages and bacon rolls that they lost count. Harold excused himself and went off to help with arrangements for the return journeys to Aletheia. Hugo and Dusty simply stayed where they were, watching people and doggedly eating food. Henrietta explored the camp and chatted to the people at the stalls, returning occasionally to Hugo and Dusty to update them on anything she had found out.

"Are you two *still* eating?" she said as she returned from another whirlwind trip around the enclosure.

"It's probably because we missed tea last night," said Hugo, excusing how much he and Dusty had eaten.

"And we missed supper too," said Dusty.

Henrietta giggled. "It doesn't seem to make much difference to the food supply," she said. "It's like the feeding of the five thousand. You two have probably eaten enough for five thousand, and there are still loads of leftovers!"

"Feeding five thousand?" queried Dusty.

"It's a reference to a story in the Bible,[27]" said Hugo. He rubbed his very full tummy.

"I think," said Dusty with his mouth full of yet another sausage, "I think that when I've learned a bit more, I would like to work in the Academy of Soldiers-of-the-Cross."

"It's a shame they won't let us join the Rescuers now," said Henrietta.

"We've still got a bit more to learn, Henry," Hugo said drily.

"I'd like to be in the Control Room," said Dusty, "like Brian."

"Not exactly like Brian, I hope," said Henrietta.

"Not exactly," said Dusty. "But I would like to help organise this!" He gestured around them, at the throngs of people, and supplies, and all sorts of bits and pieces that had somehow come together. "And I would like to get the power supply improved to the Prayer Power Monitor. Imagine defeating all your enemies with prayer like Mrs De Voté did!"

Henrietta was touched by Dusty's zeal. He had absolute

confidence that the God of the Bible, who had so recently saved him, could do anything! She felt a bit ashamed that she so often doubted.

"There's Josie!" said Henrietta. Her cousin was still pale and looked a little sheepish as she made her way through the crowd towards them. "Are you alright, Josie?" Henrietta asked kindly as Josie joined them. Josie appeared to be alright: she had brushed her hair and put on an attractive green jumper from her bag which had been recovered by a passing Rescuer and returned to her. She looked the cleanest and tidiest and most presentable of all of them.

"Of course I am," said Josie. "Why wouldn't I be?"

Henrietta sighed. She had a horrible feeling that Josie had not really changed as a result of this adventure. Josie was going back to Aletheia perhaps subdued, but she had not changed the way that Dusty so evidently had. And that meant that Henrietta's real rescue efforts must begin at home the way that Mrs De Voté had said they should all along. If Josie could not see the grace of God from the Bible, Henrietta must try to show it through her own life. Henrietta must try to help Josie. "I like your jumper," she said.

Josie stared at her cousin in some astonishment. She had long despaired of Henrietta's ignorance about fashion and clothes. "It's the latest style," she said.

"Oh," said Henrietta. She tried to think of a kind, not impatient retort. "It looks really nice on you," she said.

"I'll show you how to make one if you like," said Josie.

Henrietta forced away the horror she felt at the thought of spending her precious free time knitting with Josie. She wanted action and adventure; she had never imagined she would take up *knitting*. But she managed a smile. "Thanks, Jo," she said.

It was a big sacrifice to Henrietta and a small beginning with Josie. It was the start of her campaign to show her cousin grace and kindness. It seemed that the work of a Rescuer was not all adventure and glory: sometimes it was dealing with people who were annoying and frustrating and downright horrible; sometimes it was just patience and grace.

CHAPTER 18
THE GRAND PROCESSION

The return to Aletheia was nothing like the outward journey when they had come across so many unknown and unexpected things on the outskirts of the purple storm. The damaged Capsule Three-Sixteen was building up its power supply in the sunshine but it was not able to fly safely. It was being left in the hands of a capable engineer; it would not be taking the children home. They collected their belongings from the large, round space and took a last look at the Capsule that had played such a valiant part in the purple storm.

It was a grand procession of Rescuer vehicles that made their way from the Emergency Rendezvous and began the journey back to Aletheia. The Rescuers' engineers had rigged up a strong new crossing for the River Self. The river still raged beneath the new road but for now it had lost its danger and its power. It was swift and deep but it was also sulking. It did not grasp at the Atobs and Rescue Craft and other transportation as they trundled across. In each vehicle there were strangers who had been rescued from the storm and trusted in the Lord Jesus to save them forever[28]. Some of the people who had been rescued hadn't yet trusted in the Lord Jesus, but they wanted to go to Aletheia to learn more about what the Bible taught about the only true God[22].

Above the land transport Rescue Capsules zipped across the sky, carrying passengers swiftly to Aletheia and then returning to the Emergency Rendezvous point to pick up more. In one of these Capsules the children flew back to the Academy of Soldiers-of-the-Cross in Aletheia. They were torn between wanting to go the longer route with the land vehicles and prolonging the whole adventure, and having one more ride in the super-fast, super-smooth-flying Rescue Capsule. They weren't given the choice in any case, and no one grumbled when Harold directed them to a Capsule for their return trip.

They flew through clear, untroubled skies and straight to Aletheia. It was another sunny autumn day, and below them the land of Err looked peaceful and even pretty. Trees were turning colour and shedding leaves. From their height in the Capsule the children couldn't see the messy bits of Err, the unhappy people, the muddle of folk who were trying to live their lives without God, the many who needed to be rescued.

Very soon the majestic city of Aletheia loomed before them, clustered securely at the top of the hill in the middle of the land of Err, with the cross in the centre rising above everything else around.

"I wonder if Mum is watching the Rescue Capsules returning," said Henrietta. She peered towards their home at Foundation-of-Faith Apartments. It wouldn't have surprised her if her mother was on the balcony watching the activity in the city of Aletheia. People were dotted about the city, coming out of their houses, standing on the streets, climbing the steps to the foot of the cross to watch the procession of Rescuers and rescued people returning to Aletheia. If she had known the pilot, Henrietta might have dared to request that the Capsule fly one last lap around the city. But the Rescuer flying them home was not Bourne; Bourne was busy elsewhere. The Rescuer who flew them home was called 'Les'. He was a formidable-looking man who didn't have much to say to the children and seemed uncomfortable in their presence. He only spoke to Harold. Henrietta could just imagine how mortified Hugo would be if she asked Les the pilot to do an extra turn around the city so she could look longer at the sights below.

The Capsule hovered and lowered smoothly onto the Landing Pad at the Academy of Soldiers-of-the-Cross. It was almost disappointing how ordinary the flight had been. They were safely back in Aletheia. It was as if the purple storm had never been.

Despite the fact that there were so many people, and Rescuers, and vehicles all returning to Aletheia, the Academy of Soldiers-of-the-Cross was orderly and all of the Rescuers the children saw, as Harold led them from the Landing Pad and through the Academy, seemed to know exactly what they were doing and where they should be. There was a definite buzz of excitement around them, but it was organised excitement.

"We've got a debriefing in the Control Room," said Harold. "And then you're free to go home and get some rest, and get tided up too!"

Henrietta imagined they must all look pretty grimy and messy, except Josie who had once more tidied herself in front of a mirror on the return flight.

"What's the debriefing about?" asked Hugo, pleased that they were still involved in 'official' business at the Academy. He had been dreading being left in the Relaxation Room or being sent home. He didn't want to miss out on the excitement of the influx of strangers, and the procession of Rescue Vehicles, and all the talk and chatter about the purple storm.

"Well, it's a debriefing with Brian Buffer the Manager. Brian wants to ask you a few details regarding your call to the Control Room when you requested their assistance."

"We were really just asking them for advice," said Hugo. "I don't think there will be much to talk about."

"I'm not sure Brian sees it that way," said Harold rather drily. "He likes to debrief and gather all the relevant details after a mission – to see if they can improve their procedures for future missions. Brian likes procedures."

Henrietta groaned slightly. But she didn't really mind. She liked the Control Room with all of its incredible machines. She wouldn't mind being there for hours watching the Prayer Power Monitor, seeing what showed in the Storm Tracker Indicator glass, watching the weather change in the Weather Guide – and so many other things she hadn't had time to look at on their last visit there.

"Come to think of it, I still haven't heard how Capsule Three-Sixteen came to land at the Emergency Rendezvous," said Harold.

"Uh, well…" said Hugo, wondering how on earth they would explain that.

"It was prayer," said Dusty. "God did it." Dusty was looking forward to another visit to the Control Room. He wanted to ask Brian if he could get a Saturday job there.

"Do I need to be at the debriefing?" asked Josie. She sounded weary and was still very pale.

"Uh, no, Josie, I don't suppose you do," said Harold kindly. "I don't think you have anything to say that the others can't say for you, do you?"

Harold clearly realised that the debriefing was likely to be embarrassing for Josie who had caused the call to the Control Room by her disappearance. And Josie hadn't even been there when the Capsule had so mysteriously taken flight and landed at the Emergency Rendezvous.

Josie said a subdued goodbye to them. Harold knew she would be safe with her family in Aletheia. There was nothing to worry about; but somehow it was hard not to worry about Josie.

Harold and the three remaining children stood once more by the spiral stairs and climbed aboard the Stair-Gobbler for the ride to the Central Control Room.

"After the ride in the Capsule and the purple storm the Gobbler feels just fine," declared Henrietta after they had spun crazily up the stairs and staggered out before the large door that said, 'Central Control Room'.

That wasn't quite true. They still felt as if their insides were all upside down and that there was at least the faint possibility they might be sick in the 'Sick Here Please' bucket. But they had recovered by the time they walked onto the Observer Deck balcony. And when they once more looked down on the clanking, whirring, clicking, clacking, gurgling machines, they forgot all about the ride on the Gobbler.

Brian, in his long, white coat and minus his bright orange cardigan, was busy overseeing the massive Mission Detector screen where a swarm of people in bright yellow coats were monitoring the big rescue operation which was still making its way steadily to the safety of Aletheia. All of the Rescuers were somewhere on that huge screen. All accounted for, all being tracked, all of the vehicles watched. There were still many Rescuers elsewhere in Err too; still plenty of Rescue Vehicles to keep an eye on; still plenty of storms brewing and trouble coming – although there was no purple storm on the horizon this time.

Harold picked up the speaking tube from beside the communication screen on the balcony.

"Uh, Brian?" he said. "Harold Wallop here for the two o'clock briefing you requested. With me are Hugo and Henrietta Wallop, and Dusty Addle who were all involved in the incident you wanted to ask them about."

'Incident' made it all sound forbiddingly official, but Brian didn't look particularly intimidating. He looked tired and rumpled and uninspiring. Henrietta thought that probably Brian hadn't been home to sleep throughout the whole of the purple storm. She felt sorry for him.

Brian retrieved a speaking tube and looked up at Harold on the balcony. "Take the Leveller down and meet me in my office," he said.

"Awesome!" said Dusty.

And it was pretty cool. They were going down into the Control Room itself.

CHAPTER 19
BRIAN AND THE DEBRIEF

The Leveller was simply a moving platform which carried people from one level to another. In this instance it took the children from the Observer Deck to the Control Room where Brian's office was located. Harold and the three children stood on a round patch which was marked with a red circle on the Observer Deck. Harold pressed something with his foot and a clear, plastic shield shot up from the ground and surrounded them. They descended through the floor rapidly and without warning, leaving their stomachs feeling as if they really belonged on the Observer Deck above. Hugo grabbed Dusty who looked as if he might fall from the Leveller altogether; Hugo didn't trust the clear plastic shield and it seemed to him that Dusty might land on top of a man in a yellow coat who was just about to enter the door to the toilet.

It seemed funny to find something as commonplace as a toilet located in the round wall at the edge of the Control Room. Henrietta wondered if the toilet was also round or perhaps fashioned after one of the marvellous machines which were now so close. But Hugo refused to go and look for her.

"Well I can't go and see!" she said. "They're the men's toilets! There aren't any ladies' toilets here, are there?"

"I expect there are ladies' toilets somewhere," said Dusty peaceably. "I see a lady in a raincoat over there."

"You're just being silly, Henry," said Hugo. "We're here on important business! We can't ask to see the toilets!"

"I'll look later, alright?" said Dusty.

"Thanks, Dusty," said Henrietta with dignity. "I just wondered if the toilets have coloured smoke or do something weird," she added defensively to Hugo.

They had attracted the attention of a green coated man who was pressing buttons on the Weather Guide machine which was nearest to the children.

"Where are you checking the weather?" asked Henrietta.

"Henry!" hissed Hugo, mortified that his twin was acting as if she didn't have a clue when he, Hugo, was hoping that the adults around them assumed they were on important, official Rescuer business. One day he wanted to be here dressed in a smart uniform, just like Harold, knocking on the door of Brian's office as if he had come to report an important mission. One day…

"We're…uh…"

"Perhaps it's confidential," suggested Dusty. He had followed Henrietta towards the large clear globe that held weather. Just now it was blank and clear.

"N-no…n-not confidential…" stuttered the man, who was somewhat perplexed to be quizzed by schoolchildren in the middle of a most harassing day.

"It's snowing!" exclaimed Henrietta. "Look Hugo…I mean Dusty."

Snow was indeed drifting down from the top of the round globe, which had turned a dark grey, full of clouds and foreboding. They were real snowflakes! They began to settle on the bottom of the globe and then swirl around, quickly forming pretty drifts.

"Is it a storm somewhere in Err?" asked Henrietta.

"We're checking the forecast for the Mountains of Destruction," the man said. On the whole he was quite pleased with the interruption.

"Ready, Henry?" said Hugo. "Dusty? Brian…I mean Mr Buffer…will see us now."

"I wanted to ask the man if he could tell if we'll get snow for Christmas in Aletheia," said Henrietta regretfully as she and Dusty came away from the Weather Guide.

They followed Harold and Hugo into Mr Buffer's office. It had 'Manager' stamped on the door in big silver letters. But it was not the impressive, comfortable office that might have been expected for the 'manager' of the vast complexities of the Control Room. It was the most cluttered and disorganised room Henrietta had ever seen – and that included her own! If her mum could see this room – well, what she would say about it would take some considerable time. There might have been seats in the room, but, if there were, they were so hopelessly buried beneath papers, and files, and boxes, and all sorts of other paraphernalia, that they were completely invisible.

"I'm afraid there aren't seats for you all," said Brian. "But if you wouldn't mind…" he was tidying the rumpled camp bed which stood, somewhat incongruously, in the corner of the office. He straightened the sleeping bag, patted the pillow – which had no effect on it whatsoever – and threw the bright orange knitted cardigan which was strewn upon it into a corner against the wall. "It's been a busy couple of days," said Brian. He looked so weary and tired that Henrietta felt very sorry for him. It seemed clear that Brian had not left his office and the Control Room from the moment the purple storm was discovered.

The three children sat on the camp bed and Harold perched

on the edge of the desk. Brian removed some papers from the only visible chair which was behind the desk and sank into it. It creaked beneath him.

"I wanted this debriefing because of the unforeseen and, uh, unresolved matter regarding, uh, Rescuer Personnel protocol which occurred during your time with Capsule Three-Sixteen," said Brian. "Specifically at 2100 hours on the night of the purple storm."

"What's he talking about?" whispered Henrietta to Hugo. It was pretty safe to whisper because Brian, perhaps not knowing how to debrief three schoolchildren, directed all of his remarks at Harold.

"He's talking about Josie going missing and our call to the Control Room," murmured Hugo.

"Oh," muttered Henrietta, "why didn't he just say so?"

"We at the Control Centre, and I, the Manager, in particular, establish protocols, procedures, policies and processes in order to safeguard and protect our Rescuer Personnel. Where there are no, uh, adequate procedures for the circumstances, we, uh, in a debriefing such as this, uh, analyse the reasons for the, uh, potential inadequacy, and draw up the necessary new protocols, procedures, processes…"

"Umm…does it make a difference if no Rescuer Personnel are involved in the circumstances?" asked Hugo.

Brian swivelled his chair around to face the three children. "This is quite, uh, unforeseen," he said. "We may need to consider, uh, new protocols, procedures…"

"I think I see what's happened," said Harold. "This was really a one-off occurrence. I don't think we need concern ourselves with developing…procedures for something that may never happen again, do we?"

Brian frowned. "Of course, your opinion is valued, Private Wallop," he said, "but I have the responsibility of ensuring the safety and protection of Rescuers in the field, insofar as their liaison with the Control Room is concerned."

"I see," said Harold politely.

As interesting as Brian's office was on first acquaintance, Henrietta was already bored with talk about procedures and protocols. She had no notion how Brian could devise any procedure that would have enabled Hugo to know what to do about Josie, and really she wanted to see how high the snow in the Weather Guide had reached, and so many of the other things that lay beyond the shut door. "Why don't you just tell Mr Buffer what happened?" she suggested to Hugo. "That might help, mightn't it?"

"Uh, yes, indeed," said Brian. "I was just coming to that." He took off his large glasses and rubbed them on the edge of his grubby, white coat.

Henrietta ignored Harold's glare of annoyance at what their mother would certainly have called impertinence, and focussed innocently on the overflowing bookcase on the far wall.

"You made your call to the Control Room at 2100 hours," said Brian, reaching for a pen and opening a fresh page on a notepad.

"Uh, I really don't remember the time," said Hugo.

"I'm sure it was about then, wasn't it, Dusty?" said Henrietta.

"2103 hours to be precise," said Dusty, astonishing them all.

Henrietta giggled and then cupped her hand over her mouth. "Sorry," she said, "I thought he was joking!" Harold glared at her again; she could just see it out of the corner of her eye.

"You requested at that time the procedure for dealing with a disappearance, uh, specifically relating to Miss Josie Faithful who was part of the, uh, Rescuer Personnel on Capsule Three-Sixteen," said Brian. "Is that correct?"

"Uh, I think so," said Hugo.

Henrietta was near to laughing again so she tried to think of tragic things, like Mrs De Voté dying and all the prayer vanishing from the world. The urge to giggle quickly subsided.

"At that time we didn't have a procedure that, uh, answered to that particular predicament," said Brian. "Is that correct?"

"Yes, that's *definitely* correct," said Hugo. Henrietta had to think of sad things all over again; she just felt like laughing hysterically at this whole weird debrief thing in Brian's cluttered bedroom-cum-office. She began to wonder whether there was a Mrs Brian Buffer at all; perhaps Brian lived in the office the whole time and never left; perhaps his sister had knitted that orange cardigan.

Brian was talking about the need to establish a procedure that would assist Rescuers should this 'eventuality' – Josie disappearing – ever arise again. Henrietta looked around the paper-filled office and imagined that all of the books, and files, and tonnes of individual bits of information contained random procedures about things that might never happen again.

"On a scale of zero to ten, with zero being least likely to happen, and ten being..."

"...the most likely to happen," murmured Dusty earnestly, which just about set Henrietta going again until she imagined Hugo drowning in the River Self.

"...what would you say is the likelihood of this circumstance of, uh, Miss Faithful's disappearance happening again?" asked Brian solemnly.

"Zero," said Hugo equally solemnly.

Henrietta was intrigued to see he was not scribbling in a random pad of paper at all; he was completing an 'Incident Reporting' form.

"Zero," repeated Brian.

"Zero," said Hugo emphatically.

"We've never had a 'zero' before," said Brian. After a moment's hesitation, he wrote it on his form. "In the event of a 'zero'," Brian was reading some small print at the back of his pad, "officers are not required to proceed with the development of a new procedure. Well, I never! This has never happened before!"

Henrietta heaved a sigh of relief and noticed that Harold was grinning, and then he quickly straightened his expression into solemnity again.

"That's good," said Harold.

"We had to go through the necessary process for reporting incidents," explained Brian.

"Quite," said Harold. "Very good of you to see the kids about this yourself."

"Not at all, not at all," said Brian.

"But we won't waste anymore of your valuable time," said Harold.

"Uh, can I just ask something, sir?" said Dusty.

His use of the word 'sir' clearly pleased Brian. "Of course, my boy!" he said warmly.

"I've just become a Christian," said Dusty. "I'd really like to help in the Control Room and start to learn about the machines. I just wondered if I could come in on Saturdays and help? I don't mind clearing up and just watching…"

"Excellent!" said Brian. "Quite excellent! We can always use a willing pair of hands, and a new Christian is sometimes the most willing!"

"Well done, Dusty!" said Harold.

"You can start with cleaning up and such," said Brian. "There's always something to be done. Last week we had a blizzard in the Mountains of Destruction which escaped from the Weather Guide and filled part of the Control Room with three feet of snow!"

"Wow!" said Henrietta her eyes aglow. "I wonder if I could also...ow!" she glared at Hugo who had just pinched her.

"You'd be helping here for all of the wrong reasons!" whispered Hugo. "This is Dusty's thing. Let him get on with it!"

They followed Harold from Brian's office and back through the Control Room once more. Disappointingly, the pretty snow in the Weather Guide ball had turned to sleet, and the drifts which had been accumulating at the bottom of the globe were mush.

"But I expect there will be three feet of escaped snow for you to shovel next Saturday, Dusty!" said Henrietta encouragingly.

"Look at the Prayer Power Monitor," said Dusty. "It's close to Good!"

"People always pray more when there's some disaster, like the purple storm," said Harold as he led them back to the Leveller. "But unfortunately the prayer cover soon dies down again when the excitement is over. But you've got your eyes fixed on the right thing, Dusty. We need all the prayer we can get! You'll do a good job here."

Henrietta was ashamed that she had been thinking of snow when there was something as great as prayer to consider. "If I'm ever caught in another purple storm," she said, "I hope it's you at the end of the line in the Control Room, Dusty!"

"I'm surprised Mr Buffer didn't ask us about that Risk Assessment for minors he was talking about when we contacted the Control Room," said Hugo.

"Risk Assessment?!" exclaimed Harold, suddenly remembering. He glanced hastily over his shoulder to where Brian was talking to a man in a red coat. Any moment Brian might remember he had not asked about the Risk Assessment. "Quickly," urged Harold. "Let's go!"

CHAPTER 20
AT THE CROSS

Hugo, Henrietta and Dusty left the Academy of Soldiers-of-the-Cross and walked homewards through the busy streets of Aletheia. The sun was sinking in the sky and the chill of a frosty night was descending on the city. It had been a very long day but the city was not yet ready for rest. There was an air of excitement in Aletheia: people were coming to the city because they had trusted in the Lord Jesus or because they wanted to know more about Him.

Hugo and Henrietta took Dusty to the cross. There were numerous people already standing in Redemption Square but there was still plenty of room for them. There was always room by the cross.

For the first time Dusty saw the cross as it really was: the centre of everything. It divided history: the death and resurrection of the Lord Jesus was the most important event in the world. It presented the only way to be right before God[5] and find true, lasting peace. It demanded that people make the most vital decision of their lives: to accept or reject God's only offer of salvation.

"To think that I thought I could figure out everything myself," said Dusty. "I can't wait to tell my family what God has done for us, and how much grace He has shown to bring us back to Him."

Henrietta thought about her cousin, Josie. She needed to be kind and forgive Josie all the wrong things she said and did, even when she didn't deserve it. That was what grace was about[19]. Grace was exactly what God had shown to Henrietta when He had forgiven her sins; grace was what Henrietta must learn to show Josie.

"I hope your family come to Aletheia, Dusty," said Henrietta.

"I hope so too," said Dusty. "My brother Webb says the Academy of Science-Explains-All thinks the answers can all be found by scientific analysis; they don't believe in God at that Academy. And my brother Tumble says that the Strictly Training Academy teaches that people need lots of rules and discipline, and then they can be good enough and live in peace. They don't teach that people need to be saved by trusting in God's way of salvation."

"People want to believe they can fix things themselves," said Hugo.

"I don't think anyone wants to admit they're wrong," said

Dusty. "And if we believe what the Bible says, then that's the very first thing you have to do, isn't it? You have to admit that you are wrong, and that only God is right! Isn't faith in God such an awesome thing?"

Henrietta giggled inadvertently. "Sorry," she said. "I just like the way you say things, Dusty."

"You've lived by faith for a long time, I expect," said Dusty. "But it's new to me, and just…well, awesome! Imagine it being as simple as having confidence that what God has said and done is true! And then you just rely on that!"

"I don't think there's anything about God that makes it impossible for people to believe in Him, even when they can't actually see Him," said Hugo. "God has proved how great He is in Creation and by keeping the promises He has made in the Bible."

"Faith is the thing that connects us to God," said Henrietta reflectively. "It's like an invisible link."

"You're getting pretty wise in your old age, Henry," said Hugo.

"Faith brings the future within the present and makes the invisible seen," said Henrietta. Hugo looked at her in astonishment and she giggled. "That's a quote from Mrs Steady's lesson," she said.

"It always surprises me the things you actually learn, Henry," said Hugo.

"Thanks," she said, "I think!"

Hugo and Henrietta left Dusty at the cross and walked homewards to Foundation-of Faith Apartments. Many of the shops were closing for the night but a light shone brightly from the Faithful shop on the Fruit-of-the-Spirit shopping parade. Henrietta could see Mrs De Voté sitting in her chair behind the counter as if she had no intention of shutting up her shop. More unusually there was another lady with her, tidying Mrs De Voté's shop. Henrietta recognised this lady as Mrs Gracie who ran the Kindness shop further down the row.

"You go on," Henrietta said to Hugo. "I want to talk to Mrs De Voté."

Hugo walked on and Henrietta opened the door to the shop. The bell tinkled above the door and Mrs De Voté looked up with a smile.

"So, you returned safely from the purple storm, Henrietta," she said.

Henrietta nodded. Mrs De Voté looked pale and ill and worn. "Have you been ill, Mrs De Voté?" she asked. For, while she, Henrietta, had returned from the storm unharmed, it looked as if Mrs De Voté had been through a storm and not escaped unscathed.

"I'm a little tired, dear," said Mrs De Voté.

"She's been worn out by the storm," said Mrs Gracie.

"By the storm?" echoed Henrietta. Mrs De Voté had been nowhere near the storm!

"Praying that your faith wouldn't fail," said Mrs Gracie. She beamed on Henrietta and held out the packet of sweets that she usually offered to everyone she met.

"Uh, thanks," said Henrietta, taking a strawberry one. "Have you been praying all the time?" she asked Mrs De Voté. She now realised why Mrs De Voté looked so pale, and ill, and creased, and worn.

"She's been praying all the time," said Mrs Gracie.

Henrietta stared at the little old lady whose prayers had

sustained and protected them in the midst of the storm; who had battled and fought for them in prayer while they bumbled their way through a rescue mission on an unexpected adventure. To think that she, Henrietta, had even wondered at using the tatty knitted blue patch! The knitted square had seemed so insignificant in the face of the purple storm. But it proved so full of power!

"Did you know it would work so well?" asked Henrietta.

"What would work so well, dear?" asked Mrs De Voté.

"The knitted patch, the prayer pledge you gave me, did you know how powerful it would be?"

"I didn't even know you had used it at all, my dear," said Mrs De Voté. "We don't always know if or when our prayers have been answered. Sometimes we never know that our prayers have been answered."

"But you pray anyway?"

"I pray because the God of Heaven answers prayer,[29]" said Mrs De Voté. "And how and when He chooses to answer prayer is up to Him. He knows best."

"But you can be absolutely certain of one thing: that if you pray in the will of God – that is according to the principles of the

Bible – God answers prayer!" added Mrs Gracie. "And sometimes, in His great kindness, He lets us see the answer too."

"I hope I learn to pray like that," said Henrietta earnestly.

"It's not a gift, dear; prayer is just acting out faith in God. And you had to do your bit too. Didn't I tell you before you left for your mission in the storm? You must do your bit."

"I wasn't exactly sure what that meant," admitted Henrietta.

"Tut, tut," murmured Mrs Gracie with good humour. "Why don't young people just ask if they don't know?"

"You must be ready to be used by God in every situation," explained Mrs De Voté. "If you're not in the right condition to be used, then my prayers might be far less effective."

"Oh," said Henrietta.

"It's as simple as that," added Mrs Gracie cheerfully.

Henrietta thought about the stone she had catapulted from the knitted square. She had sent it with desperate prayer towards the worst horror of the purple storm. And that, combined with Mrs De Voté's faithful, constant prayers, had shattered the darkness and surrounded them with such wonderful calm.

"Uh, how was it…how was it your prayers were so powerful though?" asked Henrietta. "I mean, they blew away the evil and protected us from it all!" It wasn't a very accurate description of their adventure but Mrs De Voté didn't seem to mind.

"Did God do that?" she said dreamily.

"Your prayers did it too," said Henrietta.

"The strength of prayer is not in the person who prays but in the God in whom we can so completely trust!" said Mrs De Voté. "You can rely on God to do anything that He says He will do!"

"I'll try," said Henrietta.

"Faith in God is really just the certainty that what God says is true, and that what God promises will come to pass. The Bible says that if we ask for something in the will of God, then God will answer prayer[30]. So act as if what God says is absolutely certain; pray in the will of God; and expect an answer!"

"Thank you for praying for us," said Henrietta. "That's really what I came to say. I just forgot when I saw you looking so ill!"

"What a nice girl to come and thank you, Gladys!" exclaimed Mrs Gracie. She pressed another sweet into Henrietta's hand.

"I'm glad you came to tell me," said Mrs De Voté. "Now I can go and rest."

CHAPTER 21
THE NEXT ADVENTURE

Darkness had fallen on the city of Aletheia when Henrietta left Mrs De Voté's Faithful shop. She walked slowly up the street towards her home at Foundation-of-Faith Apartments. Frost was nipping in the air and the plants in Mr Forbear's crowded window boxes were already withering at the edges. Henrietta stopped and removed the head of a dead flower. Probably Mr Forbear had had another cheerful, busy day at his Patience shop and hadn't noticed the withering flowers. Probably he had been too busy talking to people passing, or trying to find the things that his customers wanted in his cluttered shop; or he might have spent all his time teaching Hilda Hasty about shop keeping in Aletheia. Henrietta wondered how Hilda was getting on. Perhaps she would return to school cheerful and patient.

Maybe Autumn Week was intended to reform them all. Dusty would return to school a different person. He completely changed his outlook when he became a Christian. Hugo was just Hugo. He was steady, constant, slowly improving in Christian life and growing stronger in the things that really mattered. Henrietta knew that she was not like that. She must strive to pray, and work at influencing and reaching and rescuing those around her, no matter how trying this might be. And she must start with Josie. She very much doubted that her cousin would return to school reformed. Henrietta must be one of those who showed her how much she needed the grace of God and the salvation He offered through the Lord Jesus.

Above the city the stars were showing in the night sky. Outside Foundation-of-Faith Apartments the flower pots had been cleared of withering summer flowers and were bright with autumn pansies.

Soon it would be winter. In a few weeks it would be Christmas, with all the excitement of the Christmas missions going out into the land of Err. Perhaps it would even snow.

Henrietta walked into the warm entrance of Foundation-of-Faith Apartments.

And she stopped abruptly in utter astonishment: in the foyer, talking to Hugo, as if he had just stepped out of the old fashioned elevator, stood their friend Jack Merryweather. And if it wasn't odd enough to see Jack suddenly with them in Aletheia, he seemed to be wearing his pyjamas too!

"Jack!" gasped Henrietta. "What are you doing here …?!" She gazed at Jack from head to bare toes. Jack might be wearing his pyjamas, but he hadn't put on his slippers.

"I was in bed at home having a dream," said Jack, evidently thinking this was adequate explanation for his strange attire.

"Is this your dream?" asked Henrietta.

"It might be," said Jack.

"But we're not asleep," said Henrietta.

"I think we know that, Henry," said Hugo.

"Are you staying?" asked Henrietta, still staring at Jack as if she couldn't quite believe he was really and truly there with them.

"He can't stay," said Hugo.

Jack glanced at the special spy watch he wore on his wrist.

It was a good job he hadn't removed it last night when he went to bed. It was a very useful watch. It didn't only show the time, it gave him lots of other information too. "I've got to go soon," said Jack.

"Go soon!" echoed Henrietta. "But we've got loads to catch up on! And we must tell him all about the purple storm!"

"We've been catching up," said Hugo. "I told him about the purple storm. I'll tell you all about Jack's news later."

"Uh…how's Timmy?" asked Henrietta.

"He's alright," said Jack. He thought that probably Henrietta wanted to know more than that, but he didn't know what else to say. His watch gave a short beep. "Look," he said. And he removed his watch and held it out to Henrietta.

Henrietta took the watch and looked at the screen. The watch showed a written message. The message said '*Time to go home*'.

"But how do you get back home again?" asked Henrietta.

Jack shrugged. He didn't usually

panic over practicalities, and there certainly didn't seem to be any point in worrying when it all felt like a dream.

"I think he's meant to take the elevator," said Hugo. He pointed to the indicator on the wall. Usually it told you how far the elevator could take you. But this time it said, *'Passenger Jack Merryweather: ready to go.'*

"Oh," said Henrietta. "Will you come back soon, Jack?"

"I think so," said Jack. He stepped into the elevator and for a moment they all looked at one another.

"Come back in time for Christmas," said Henrietta.

"I'll try," said Jack.

"Oh, I almost forgot to tell you!" said Hugo. "We ate the sandwiches you left the last time you were here! They tasted a bit weird!"

"They had marmite in them!" said Jack.

And then, oddly, the doors of the elevator closed without any prompting, and Jack vanished from their sight.

Hugo and Henrietta stood for a moment in stunned silence.

"Was that all a dream?" Henrietta asked at last.

"I don't think so," said Hugo. "I expect it's just something that can happen…you know, when people come and go from other places, like Jack's country."

"I don't think we really know that can happen," said Henrietta.

"Well, he's been here before," said Hugo reasonably. "All sorts of people come from all sorts of places to Aletheia!"

"What's *marmite?*" asked Henrietta.

Hugo shrugged. "Something they have in Jack's country," he said.

"Well, that's the bit I *did* know actually," said Henrietta. "I just wondered what they put in it!"

"Perhaps they make marmite from the sick in the Vomitorium at the Academy," said Hugo.

Henrietta giggled, and then they both watched in silence as the elevator once more arrived at their level – from wherever it had gone with Jack – and slowly the doors unfolded.

The elevator was empty.

"Shall we…?" asked Henrietta hesitantly.

The twins walked towards the elevator. It looked normal, and it felt normal as they stepped inside and sank onto the cushioned seats for the ride to their own top-floor apartment.

"I thought that perhaps…" Henrietta sighed.

"I don't think it will take us to Jack's country, Henry," said Hugo.

And he was right. The elevator reading no longer said anything about Jack being a passenger. Instead it simply said 'All the way to the top'.

And it took them home again.

EPILOGUE

When Jack Merryweather awoke he still remembered his dream. It had seemed so real. He had spoken to his friends Hugo and Henrietta Wallop; he remembered the feel of the soft cushioned seat of the old fashioned elevator; he had smelled supper cooking in one of the ground floor homes in Foundation-of-Faith Apartments. He wished he had gone outside the apartment block and into Aletheia, even if it was only a dream. He would like to have seen his friend Hezekiah Wallop again too. He wished that Timmy had been with him.

Would he and Timmy ever go back to Aletheia properly, the way they had gone before? Somehow he felt that they would.

Meanwhile, it was probably time to get ready for school. It was a shame he wasn't in Aletheia right now having an adventure, instead of going to school. Jack looked at his wrist to check the time. His special spy watch wasn't there so he reached for it on his bedside table.

But his watch was gone.

He had left it in Aletheia.

REFERENCES

Unless otherwise stated, all Bible references are taken from the New King James Version of the Bible.

1.   [References on pages 9, 16, 47] You can read about this adventure in Book 1 of the Aletheia Adventure Series, The Rescue of Timmy Trial.

2.   [Reference on page 24] The message of the gospel [that is, the good news about salvation], is that the Lord Jesus came into the world to save people.

A verse about this is found in **1 Timothy 1:15**:

"This is a faithful saying and worthy of all acceptance, that Christ Jesus came into the world to save sinners."

3.   [Reference on page 24] There are many verses in the Bible that explain how to become a Christian. Here are a couple of examples:

Acts 16:31:

"Believe on the Lord Jesus Christ, and you will be saved."

Romans 10:9:

"If you confess with your mouth the Lord Jesus and believe in your heart that God has raised Him from the dead, you will be saved."

4.   [Reference on page 24] 'Sin' is the Bible name for all the wrong things that everyone has done. The Bible teaches that everyone has sinned against God.

There is a verse about this in **Romans 3:23**:

"For all have sinned and fall short of the glory of God."

5.   [References on pages 30, 37, 171, 213] The Bible teaches that there is only one way to be right with God, and that is through the Lord Jesus. The Lord Jesus is the mediator – that is, He brings God and people together, and brings people back to God. This is explained in **1 Timothy 2:5**:

"For there is one God and one Mediator between God and men, the Man Christ Jesus."

[Note that 'men' here means all people]

The Lord Jesus also said that He was the way back to God.

This can be found in **John 14:6**:

"Jesus said to him, "I am the way, the truth, and the life. No one comes to the Father except through Me.""

6.   [Reference on page 36] The Bible teaches that everyone has sinned (see point 4 above) and that the reason we sin is that we are fundamentally wrong inside and have been ever since Adam sinned in the Garden of Eden and sin entered into the world. The Bible often calls the inside part of a person – the

part that thinks, and plans, and feels – the heart. A verse about this can be found in **Jeremiah 17:9**:

"The heart is deceitful above all things,

And desperately wicked;

Who can know it?"

7. [Reference on page 45] When we trust in the Lord Jesus, He washes us clean from everything we have done wrong. This is explained in **1 John 1:7**:

"And the blood of Jesus Christ His [God's] Son cleanses us from all sin."

8. [Reference on page 45] The Lord Jesus did not come into the world to condemn the world. A reference to this is found in **John 3:17**:

"For God did not send His Son into the world to condemn the world, but that the world through Him might be saved."

9. [Reference on page 48] 'Peace I leave with you' is a reference to a verse in the Bible in which the Lord Jesus is speaking. This is in **John 14:27**:

"Peace I leave with you, My peace I give to you; not as the world gives do I give to you. Let not your heart be troubled, neither let it be afraid."

10.   [Reference on page 48] The Bible teaches that the Lord Jesus
        came into the world to bring peace (see also point 9 above).
        People can receive peace with God when they trust in the Lord
        Jesus. A verse about this is:

        Romans 5:1:

        "Therefore, having been justified by faith, we have peace with
        God through our Lord Jesus Christ."

11.   [Reference on page 49] Faith is defined in the Bible in **Hebrews
        11:1**:

        "Now faith is the substance of things hoped for, the evidence
        of things not seen."

        "Now faith is the assurance of things hoped for, the conviction
        of things not seen."

        [English Standard Version]

        "Now faith is confidence in what we hope for and assurance
        about what we do not see."

        [New International Version]

12.   [Reference on page 49] In **Hebrews chapter 11** the Bible
        shows the results of faith in God. The Bible never teaches that
        we should have faith in anyone but God, because God alone
        cannot fail. (See also point 13 on the next page, which shows
        why people should only trust in God).

13. [References on pages 49, 134, 157, 170] The Bible is full of reasons why God alone should be trusted. Here are a few examples of reasons to trust in God:

    a. God is our Creator and designed us to be in communion with Him and to trust in Him (Genesis chapters 1 and 2);

    b. God is above all and rules over everything (Psalm 83:18; Psalm 92:8; Daniel 4:17);

    c. God sees everything (Hebrews 4:13);

    d. God knows everything (Psalm 147:5);

    e. God cannot lie, and always keeps His promises (Titus 1:2; Hebrews 10:23; 2 Peter 3:9);

    f. God does not change (Malachi 3:6);

    g. God is love and always seeks the best for us (1 John 4:8; Jeremiah 31:3; John 3:16);

    h. God is faithful and has promised to forgive us on the basis of what the Lord Jesus has done (1 John 1:9).

14. [Reference on page 55] The account of the fall of the first man Adam (when sin entered the world) is found in **Genesis chapter 3**.

15. [Reference on page 80] This is a quote from a verse in the Bible, **Romans 16:27**:

"To God, alone wise, be glory through Jesus Christ forever. Amen."

16. [References on pages 96, 114, 151] The Bible talks about Christians putting on the 'armour of God'. This is explained in **Ephesians 6:10-18**:

"Finally, my brethren, be strong in the Lord and in the power of His might.

Put on the whole armour of God, that you may be able to stand against the wiles of the devil. For we do not wrestle against flesh and blood, but against principalities, against powers, against the rulers of the darkness of this age, against spiritual hosts of wickedness in the heavenly places. Therefore take up the whole armour of God, that you may be able to withstand in the evil day, and having done all, to stand.

Stand therefore, having girded your waist with truth, having put on the breastplate of righteousness, and having shod your feet with the preparation of the gospel of peace; above all, taking the shield of faith with which you will be able to quench all the fiery darts of the wicked one. And take the helmet of salvation, and the sword of the Spirit, which is the word of God; praying always with all prayer and supplication in the Spirit."

17.   [Reference on page 106] Money growing wings and flying away is a reference to

Proverbs 23:5:

"Will you set your eyes on that which is not?

For riches certainly make themselves wings;

They fly away like an eagle toward heaven."

[The Bible does not mean that money literally flies; this verse is saying that riches are easily lost.]

18.   [Reference on page 130] This is a reference to a verse in **Psalm 119:105** which explains how the Bible can show us the way as a light:

"Your word is a lamp to my feet

And a light to my path."

[The Bible doesn't mean that the Bible is a literal light; this verse is saying that the Word of God will be our guide through life if we believe what the Bible says.]

19.   [References on pages 132, 214] The Bible contains many references to the grace of God and the grace of the Lord Jesus Christ. 'Grace' means showing mercy and forgiveness when people don't deserve it. Here are some examples of the God of grace in the Bible:

John 1:17:

"For the law was given through Moses, but grace and truth came through Jesus Christ."

1 Corinthians 1:4:

"I thank my God always concerning you for the grace of God which was given to you by Christ Jesus."

2 Corinthians 8:9:

"For you know the grace of our Lord Jesus Christ, that though He was rich, yet for your sakes He became poor, that you through His poverty might become rich."

Ephesians 1:7:

"In Him we have redemption through His blood, the forgiveness of sins, according to the riches of His grace."

20.   [Reference on page 132] This refers to a verse from the Bible, from **Ephesians 2:8**:

"For by grace you have been saved through faith, and that not of yourselves; it is the gift of God."

21.   [References to pages 133, 173] The Bible teaches that all Scripture [i.e. all of the words in the Bible] comes from God, and therefore they are the Word of God. A verse that describes this is **2 Timothy 3:16-17**:

"All Scripture is given by inspiration of God, and is profitable for doctrine, for reproof, for correction, for instruction in righteousness, that the man of God may be complete, thoroughly equipped for every good work."

22.   [References on pages 134, 171, 194] The Bible makes it clear that there is only one God, who is our Creator. For example:

1 Corinthians 8:6:

"There is one God, the Father, of whom are all things, and we for Him; and one Lord Jesus Christ, through whom are all things, and through whom we live."

Deuteronomy 6:4:

"The Lord our God, the Lord is one!"

Ephesians 4:6:

"One God and Father of all, who is above all, and through all, and in you all."

1 Timothy 2:5:

"For there is one God and one Mediator between God and men [all people], the Man Christ Jesus."

23.   [References on pages 134, 171] This is a quote from **Psalm 46:1:**

"God is our refuge and strength,

A very present help in trouble."

24.   [References on pages 152, 173] The description "living and powerful Word of God" is a reference to **Hebrews 4:12**:

"For the word of God is living and powerful, and sharper than any two-edged sword, piercing even to the division of soul and spirit, and of joints and marrow, and is a discerner of the thoughts and intents of the heart."

25.   [Reference on page 170] The Bible says that God is light in **1 John 1:5**:

"This is the message which we have heard from Him and declare to you, that God is light, and in Him is no darkness at all."

26.   [Reference on page 187] The Bible shows that the sacrifice of the Lord Jesus, when He died upon the cross, is enough to take away all the sins in the world that have ever been committed by every single person. For example, **1 Timothy 2:5-6**:

"For there is one God and one Mediator between God and men, the Man Christ Jesus, who gave Himself a ransom for all."

However, the Bible also makes it clear that only those who trust in the Lord Jesus for salvation will be saved.

27.   [Reference to page 189] The feeding of the five thousand is a reference to a miracle that the Lord Jesus carried out when he

fed five thousand people. You can find an account of this in: **Matthew 14: 15-21; Mark 6:35-44; Luke 9:12-17; John 6:5-14**.

This is the only miracle of the Lord Jesus which is recorded in all four gospel accounts of the life of the Lord Jesus.

28. [Reference on page 193] There is a passage in the Bible that shows that once someone has trusted in the Lord Jesus, they are saved forever. This is in **John 10:28-29**:

"And I give them eternal life, and they shall never perish; neither shall anyone snatch them out of My hand. My Father, who has given them to Me, is greater than all; and no one is able to snatch them out of My Father's hand."

29. [Reference on page 218] **James 5:16-18** is a verse about God answering prayer:

"The effective, fervent prayer of a righteous man avails much. Elijah was a man with a nature like ours, and he prayed earnestly that it would not rain; and it did not rain on the land for three years and six months.

And he prayed again, and the heaven gave rain, and the earth produced its fruit."

30. [Reference on page 220] There are verses in the Bible which explain that God will answer prayer when we ask something

in keeping with His will (God's will is always in keeping with the Bible and we must live in touch with Him if we want to know His will). Here are some examples:

John 14:13-14:

"And whatever you ask in My name, that I will do, that the Father may be glorified in the Son. If you ask anything in My name, I will do it."

John 15:16:

"I chose you and appointed you that you should go and bear fruit, and that your fruit should remain, that whatever you ask the Father in My name He may give you."

1 John 3:22:

"And whatever we ask we receive from Him [God], because we keep His commandments and do those things that are pleasing in His sight."

1 John 5:14:

"Now this is the confidence that we have in Him [God], that if we ask anything according to His will, He hears us."